It's Okay

Let's Get Real About This Thing We Call Parenting

TERESA HAMILTON

Illustrated by Koraima Ortiz Garcia and
Tara Mahobi Bernard Santos

A special thanks to my dear friends and family …

Thank you, thank you for the support, encouragement and, of course, the stories. This book would not have been possible without each of you. I am beyond blessed to be surrounded by friends and family that I truly adore and who believe in me.

To my two amazing illustrators, Kory and Tara! You two are wise beyond your junior high years and your passion for art is unmatchable. Thank you for joining me on this ridiculous journey and for being so incredibly fun to work with.

To my endearing husband and obnoxiously wonderful four children, thank you for making my time with you so memorable and my life so rich. I love you all.

To my grandma, Eunice Heimes, who passed away during the final phase of publishing this book. One of the stories in this book was submitted by my father; written from the perspective of my grandma. While I am deeply saddened by her loss and that she will never see her story in print, I feel blessed to have known such an amazing woman who created a generous, loving and unified family.

It's Okay

Let's Get Real About This Thing We Call Parenting

Introduction

Parenting is hard. Parents are not prepared for the difficult journey that lies ahead when a child is born. As babies are born into the world, there is a sense of awe and wonder. There is helplessness and despair when the hope of a baby is lost. When parents get real about pregnancy, raising children and fighting to keep marriages alive, struggles become very genuine. Feelings of inadequacy, guilt and judgment overcome parents everywhere on a daily basis.

It's not easy to get 'real' about this thing people call parenting. When one gets 'real' about how hard parenting actually is, it's like admitting to failure. Life is hard enough to manage with one imperfect being. Adding a spouse, a pet, a job or a child to the mix complicates life, adds struggles and intensifies issues. No one wants to admit that they don't LOVE every minute of the life they have been blessed to have. If one gets 'real' about life and parenting, it's safe to confess that some days are REALLY difficult.

Messing up happens. The famous sayings, "Don't cry over spilled milk," "Your glass should be half full," or "Look on the bright side of things," sometimes minimize the stress that is very real in a mind or body. Messing up doesn't mean that someone cannot be a wonderful person, wife, friend, brother or aunt. Everyone will mess up. Everyone will make mistakes. Mess-ups and mistakes can lead to great growth— minus the feelings of inadequacy, guilt and judgment felt about them.

It's time to get 'real' about life. Especially about parenting! Admitting to being full of error is not easy. Parenting cannot be about proving who can do it best. Rather, it has to be about enjoying the blessings that have been given. Belief in the work being done, the life being lived and the trials that can be learned from, is what creates a life full of contentment.

Social media has made the world of parenting, well, the world of living, a constant question. Questions about self-worth and potential creep into the hearts and minds of millions. Perfection is easy to achieve through a photo or two. As one scrolls through the newsfeed or reads up on friends' latest happenings, the 'real' story is not revealed. The comparisons need to stop; no two lives are the same. The judgments need to be halted; no one can do it all. Everyone is granted strengths and given limitations. It's time to live within those parameters and stop the punishment for not being what others are. Belief in one's self, limitations and all, is a must in order to fully appreciate the blessings one is surrounded by.

No parent wakes up in the morning wondering how to best screw up his/her child. Sometimes love is all there is to offer. While there is always room for improvement, it's critical to recognize areas that are going well. Illegal activity and truly negative behavior cannot be condoned, but aside from that it's imperative to remember that everyone has limitations. These limitations can lead to great growth over time, if one is willing to learn from mistakes.

This book was created with the idea that parents, and all people really, need to be reminded of how wonderful they are, despite the self-deprivation and negative self-talk. Parents (moms especially) need to let go of the guilt, let go of the comparisons, let go of the inadequacy, live in the moment and just do the best they can. It's time to laugh and give ourselves permission to screw up. After all is said and done, most times in life, **it really is okay.**

Points To Ponder

Many brave souls contributed the stories you are about to read. These stories reveal our most human moments as parents; they range from vulnerable to joyful and everything in between. These are stories that often go untold and stories that took courage to share. Hopefully in reading about these parenting moments you will be provided some reassurance that you are definitely NOT alone in your parenting journey. You will also be provided some peace over difficult times you've had in the past or struggles lurking in your future. Settle in and be prepared to laugh, cry, commiserate and empathize with your fellow parents.

While this book is focused on the journey of parenting, the concepts within can be applied to the basic 'life' journey we all live as well. As you read the stories ahead, please keep the following points in mind.

Be Thoughtful With Your Words

People will say the darndest things. Sometimes I wonder if God only created a mental filter in half of the world's population. Most of the time I don't think people are being malicious, they just don't know what else to say. Let's be honest; we all have been in that awkward situation where our foot did not enter our mouth fast enough before the words came out. Most people in the world are good and given the opportunity to be honest, would talk realistically and caringly about any topic. So often superficial chatting leads to hurt feelings and confusion. If only we could all just get 'real' about our struggles, our feelings and our thoughts. Then maybe some of the things that others say, or even that we say, would be more thoughtful and less hurtful.

As parents, most of us really are just doing the best we can. Some days, usually the ones when we think things are actually okay, we are forced to answer an insensitive question or decipher what an unsympathetic comment actually means. Questions and comments come at you from all angles when you hope to become a parent or when you enter the parenting journey.

"I'm sure you'll get pregnant soon."

"Are you sure you're not having twins, you're SO big?"

"What a HEALTHY baby!"

"That sure is a busy boy."

"Wow, you've got your hands full!"

People are unaware of your personal struggles and sometimes your feelings. These questions and comments leave you feeling sad, fat and insecure; plus thinking that your child should be on meds.

Be thoughtful in your words. If you can't say something nice, don't say anything at all (it'd be better that way). And, if you've been caught on the other end, do your best to assume that no harm was intended. Try to let the questions and comments roll off your back. Try to provide thoughtful feedback about how comments or questions made you feel so that the person won't continue to offend others.

Don't Judge Me Just Because My Mistakes Are Different Than Yours

We all have done it; it's gotten the best of each of us. Judgment of others! Stop. We all need to stop. It's not productive and it is hurtful. No one is perfect. We all make mistakes. It's just that I make different mistakes than you do. There is really no way to fully understand what is going on in someone else's world. No way to grasp why people are making the decisions they are making. We don't know complete histories or backgrounds; we can't effectively judge why people are the way they are.

Stop the judgment. There are people in the world who are downright awful. I am not ignorant to the fact that not all people are good.

I definitely try to see the best in others, but I know that sometimes people are purposefully hurtful and mean. We don't have to join them in their negative misery. We can assume the best of others and assume that those people who are hurting others have probably been hurt more times in the past than we can comprehend. Let's do the right thing. Let's remember that we have each been blessed with gifts and strengths and we are each challenged with limitations. These differences are what make the world so wonderful.

Bad Behavior Is Not Condoned

Here is my disclaimer. This book is written for parents who mess-up, but who are working daily to be the best they can be. The saying, "It's Okay," is meant to help us through difficult moments when we feel the world has stopped spinning because of the madness we are currently in. It's meant to turn our terrible moments into, "Well, it's not as bad as I thought it was," moments.

It's not okay to physically or emotionally abuse your children. It's not okay to use drugs and alcohol in an abusive way. It's not okay to neglect your child's basic needs. These things are not okay. Please seek out the help and support you need if you are struggling from an addiction or other harmful behavior. The *Support* section at the end of the book can provide you possible resource options if you are in need of professional help.

As I was writing this book and loving my motto, "It's Okay," I began to question that there are a lot of things in life (especially in the parenting world) that are NOT OKAY! In my right conscience, I couldn't let my Points to Ponder number three go unsaid. It's a fine line, but chances are if you are reading this book, you understand that toeing the line is different than crossing it.

Perfection Is Not Possible, But Don't Give Up Trying

No one is asking you to be the perfect person or the perfect parent; that's not realistic. Take these *It's Okay* stories as an inspiration that perfection doesn't exist … but that doesn't mean you have to give up trying. Reflecting on what is working in your world and constantly trying to improve on what is not working will make you the best person and parent possible.

In talking with parents, it seemed that a common place for the most defeating moments in our parenting journey happen in church. CHURCH! This should be a place of peace. A place where we are one with GOD and our children can feel His love. HA! HA! HA! I'll look around and notice every other kid doing what they are supposed to be doing, except my kids. Who thought that just one hour a week could cause such misery? My point is that my kids will NEVER be perfect in church, but that doesn't mean that I should stop taking them or enduring my hour of hell. Once I embraced the fact that perfection was not possible at church, things didn't seem as bad. Good behavior is still expected and we try to do better every week that we go, but in giving my kids a little leeway, striving for the perfect hour has become more bearable. I've even been able to enjoy the sermon a time or two since.

As you encounter difficult moments in your journey, embrace them. Try to overcome them. Know that you are going to have challenge after challenge thrown at you in life. Take on the challenges with as much force as you have that day (some days you will have more than others). Do the best you can. Don't give up. Don't set your standard on being perfect; set your standard on a constant work in progress … one that attempts to be great, but knows that it's okay to not be perfect.

Laughter Will Soften The Tears

My husband is so embarrassing to take to funerals. The man is just awkward. If only he could kindly express his condolences, or say something like, "I'm sorry for your loss." The guy gets so uncomfortable and tells bad jokes throughout the service and then after when people are mingling. Seriously, people must think he is so insensitive (which is actually far from the truth). The truth of the matter is, his only comfort in those sad and awkward moments, is laughter.

While I apologize for him frequently, his crude jokes and inappropriate timing of comments often lighten the mood. Laughter certainly does soften the tears. At our worst moments in life, when tears are all that we have left, laughter can undoubtedly be a much-needed relief.

It's not easy to laugh at yourself. It's not easy to think of your blunders as bloopers. In the end, though, if we take time to laugh, we often feel a million times better. There will be times when it may take hours, days or years before you can laugh at a situation. But, try. It's so worth it. And when you do finally allow yourself to laugh, other people will laugh along with you and then begin to share their struggles, too. Choosing to laugh when you really want to cry will lighten your load, strengthen your heart and make your day just a little bit brighter.

Good Friends Can Make It All Better

We all need different people in our lives for different reasons. Our spouse is just one of many people that can offer us the sense of balance good friends can give us. Good friends make the challenging moments a little easier to weather. Good friends, like your spouse, love you despite your flaws. We are all stronger together than we are alone. Whether it's a 'girl's night out' or a 'beer with the brothers,' take time to foster your friendships. They will add an extra dimension and richness to your life that cannot be replaced.

We all have a front that we put on for most people. We can't get 'real' with the stranger on the corner or the co-worker that needs you to be focused while at work. Some people don't care about your struggles and don't want to hear about them. Find people who do. It's helpful, but not necessary, that these individuals have a similar situation to yours. This allows for honesty without judgment because you can understand one another.

You've got to be able to let your hair down with someone. Hopefully your hair is always down with your spouse (this is of course wishful thinking that things in your marriage are always hunky dory, which is not always the case), but outside of your home, you have to have a place to turn. Take time to build relationships and then take time to help them grow. Friendships are a must, but they don't just happen. Plant the seed, water it, give it sunlight and then continue to help it grow season after season, year after year and struggle after struggle. It's worth it.

We All Have Good Days

It's inevitable that the day you are struggling to stay above water, you will run into someone who has accomplished the world before 8:00 am. It might be your neighbor who got up and ran three miles, hit the store and had extra time to braid her daughter's hair or the friend you call that has just made her children an award winning breakfast. All this information is coming at you when you rolled out of bed late, had the fight of your life with one of your children, maintained a breakfast of cold cereal for the fourth day in a row and then sent two of your kids off to school without brushing their teeth. It's crucial on these days to remember we ALL have our good days but, we all have our bad days, too.

Not every day can be a good day. What defines a 'good' day anyway? Is it a clean house? Is it an hour long, sweat-filled work out? Is it that you survived an hour without a time-out for your three-year-old? Is it that you took an hour to sit and play with your children? The problem with 'good' days is that we have to define them for ourselves. We can't look at what others are doing or accomplishing. It has to be about what *we* want out of our day.

Stop listening to what other people are doing and wishing you could be more like them. Take time to really think about and identify the things that make you feel like your day has been one you can check off as 'good'. When others have had good days and are feeling on top of the world, be happy for them. Don't wish you could be more like them, but rather take their success and weigh that in on your list. Ask them for advice on how they accomplish the things they do. Chances are they are wishing they could be more like you in some way or another. We all have good days. Don't get so down on yourself when you don't. And try to pick out the pieces of your day that were a success—the day couldn't have been ALL bad!

You Can Be A Powerful Force

Believe it or not, you can change the world one person at a time. It's scary to think that you could be the person that lights a flame deep inside someone or who blows out the only dim light that may have been present. You can be the bright spot in a dreary day for a lonely soul or you can kick a person while he/she is down. Take time to relate with others; to smile at someone in her darkest hour. Be a powerful force in a positive way, helping others to see that they, too, can make a difference.

The next time you hear a screaming toddler in the store, don't go the other way and thank God it's not your kid. Intentionally walk by that mom and give her a knowing smile. Give her an, "I've been there; it's okay." You can't control anyone but yourself and maybe if you pass on your goodness enough, it will come back to you when you, yourself, are in a moment of despair.

I went to the most extraordinary funeral; one where I wished I would have known this special man better. Apparently he was a powerful force in more ways than one. The thing people noticed most about him was the way he approached each and every day. When asked how he was doing, he would not answer with a, "fine" or an, "okay." His response was, "I'm awesome." His smile and positive attitude turned around more people than can be counted. You do make a difference. You can change the world ... one person at a time. Be a force.

Balance Is The Key ... But What's Yours?

Balance, balance, balance; find your balance. What the heck does this mean? You hear it in every facet of your life and every time that any change or rite of passage occurs. There are so many factors to being balanced, but the challenge is that my needs are different than your needs. The battles I choose to fight won't be the same ones you choose to fight. So when people talk about finding your balance, the first piece is to understanding number one—understanding yourself and your needs.

Some of the big pieces of a balanced life will be similar for people: spirituality, health, relationships and work. These aren't all the pieces, but a good place to start. Within each of these pieces, are issues and factors that affect what balance would look like for each of them. My spiritual balance may be completely different than yours and your two hour daily run may not fit into my health plan. Balance can be achieved and maintained, but the only person who can define what your balance looks like is you.

Let's start with spirituality. Finding a place where you are at peace with your spirituality isn't as easy as rolling the dice to find a church that fits. Once you find a church, there's the piece of how much time and effort can be spent towards making your spirituality grow. Your spiritual journey or path may look completely different than mine and that's okay. Depending on your life situation, you may have hours to devote to strengthening your relationship with a higher being, while I may be at a place where I'm lucky to get in a prayer before dinner once a week.

In regards to health, there are about 95 things to consider. Weight, working out, cholesterol, medical conditions, eating healthy ... it's not like one thing is going to fix your health and make you feel more in balance with life. Finances can play a factor in this as well. Life looks a lot different for someone who can afford a personal trainer or can afford to eat only organic food. The time that goes into being healthy creates a major issue when a family is involved. Health should be a priority and will alter one's outlook dramatically, but, again, it's just not that easy. Balancing your health starts with *your* most pressing needs and then figuring out how meeting those needs will work for you.

Relationships are crucial to feeling connected, important and balanced within this big bad world we live in. But, as was mentioned earlier, relationships don't just happen. They have to be planted, watered, given sun, then watered again, then weeded, then watered again, then given more sun, then weeded again. Real relationships require real work. Money and time can greatly affect where relationships begin and end. As we go through different phases in life we can devote more time and money to the relationships in our world. There are times when returning a phone call, a text message or an e-mail would put us over the edge. We run out of gas sometimes. And there are some years when a dinner out, paying for a sitter or having a group over for dinner would destroy a budget. These are the real issues that get in the way of balancing relationships.

As you can see, balance is not something that is easily achieved. On top of trying to keep our spirituality, health and relationships intact, we are supposed to work so we have money to pay for it all. This doesn't even touch on the fact that you may be stuck in a job you don't like or that you're not good at (so maybe you have to throw more training or college into the mix). Then somehow you are supposed to find time for a hobby that makes you feel like you have something that is your own. Plus you're supposed to foster your marriage **and** spend time with your immediate family **and** read to keep up on the latest world happenings **and** stay current on local topics **and** find out how to nurture your kids' needs **and** find time to volunteer **and, and, and.**

Balance is not easily achievable. But a good start to achieving balance is to identify the priorities in your life and what might be missing from making you feel complete. Knowing yourself, what's important to you and what makes you happy will help get you on the right track. We can all do better; we can all strive for more. Taking baby steps in the right direction can make a world of difference for achieving the balance you need.

The Grass Will Continue To Always Be Greener On The Other Side

The truth of the matter is, your neighbor's lawn will continue to look better than yours, unless you water, pull the weeds and spend the time necessary to make your own healthier. It's so easy get on Facebook and witness what others are spending their time doing. This starts the endless cycle of, "I wish I …" or, "I should have …" or, "Why didn't I …?" We have to stop these comparisons. It's important to look at our own needs, our own values and our own desires. You can't do it all, be it all and then have time to post it all!

It's okay to admit to others that you can't afford what they can. It's okay to say that you're too emotionally exhausted to take on one more thing. It's okay for you to say that it's not in the cards for you right now. It's okay to admit that you're working on you. If you take time to foster your own self, your own family and your own needs—your grass will start to perk up and look a little more like your neighbors. It may not be perfect, but chances are, if you look closely at your neighbor's lawn, it has just as many flaws as yours; those flaws will just be different. Take time to appreciate who you are, what you have and the life that you have been blessed with.

CHAPTER I

I'll Never

The first chapter of our parenting journey begins before we actually become parents. Before that tiny little bean is even a twinkle in our eyes. We start this journey from the time we are old enough to judge others around us. Maybe it began for you in junior high or high school. Or maybe you were lucky enough to get to college. But for some, it began as early as age five. It might have sounded quite profound coming from your five-year-old mouth. "Oh yeah, well when I'm a parent, I'm never going to ...!" The list is endless.

We truly are the PERFECT parents before we actually encounter the parenting experience. There are many parents who wish that they would have kept their mouths shut before they were technically parents. Many who wish they could eat their words or take them back long before they knew what the parenting world was actually going to be like. Oh, the things we will say. Even to our spouse. "Honey, when we have kids, we will never ...!" Whether you were a spirited child who knew better than your parents, a skilled babysitter who had all the tricks, or just an average Joe, we have all spoken those terrible two words we can never take back (until it's too late). I'll Never.

How does that saying go? "You should never, say, never." It's so true. You don't really know what it's like until you've been there, until you've actually gone through what others have gone through. Whether a person is single or raising a family of 10, it's not fair to judge. Who knows if someone they love just died, or they were up all night with a sick child, or they have more on their plate than you can see. It's scary because you don't really know. If you are a parent, you don't even know how that second or third or fourth, etc. kid is going to turn out (more than likely, not like your first). If you've been a sucker, judged someone a time or two, or used those two dreadful words, it's okay. We all live and learn. We can all develop new habits and understand more today than we did yesterday.

As a parent, I'll never
… let an unruly child write all over the wall
… let our child sleep in our bed
… let my baby eat off the disgusting floor
… put my baby's pacifier back in her mouth before cleaning it
… resort to soap or vinegar or tabasco sauce
… hire a cleaning lady
… send my kids out in dirty, disgusting clothes
… have snotty-nosed kids
… let my kids go out with crazy hair that hasn't been brushed
… let my kid wear pajamas in public
… let my child play in the garbage
… lock my kid in the car
… yell like that at my kids

What's your 'I'll Never'? Watch out before you let those two little nasty words roll off your tongue. You, too, may someday have to eat those precious words of things you said you'd never do.

Super Spanker

I'll never ... spank my children!

Let me just start this story by disclosing the fact that I have five children, one of which has special needs. Oh, and they are all under the age of eight. Saying I am busy at this point is an understatement. I am in a perpetual state of what I like to refer to as, 'placenta brain'. If it weren't for my kids, who I love more than anything, maybe I'd be somewhat sane and organized. Or is this wishful thinking? The saying, *the grass is always greener on the other side*, is one that I try to remind myself of often.

When I was growing up, my folks were continuously caught saying, "You know this hurts me more than it hurts you." Yes, I am referring to spankings. I got them like crazy growing up. Nightly, if I'm being honest! Spanking, in my opinion isn't easy to do. Thinking I wouldn't need to resort to spanking (pre-children), I now realize what my parents meant. My family combination is deadly; having a house full of young children that include the 'payback offspring' I received from torturing my own parents, feels like more than I can handle some days.

Not only have I resorted to spanking in my own family, but my kids have now, on a couple occasions, gotten the 'double spanking'. This is when *Mommy Dearest's* buttons have been pushed so far that she has to use both hands to spank two kids at one time. I'm sure if you were a fly on the wall watching this, it would be better than a five-star comedy show. Now I can't say that it hurts me more than them because in that moment I am so insane that I'm not thinking.

Sad to say, after all is said and done, the 'double spanking' method doesn't work. I maybe get a reaction that forces a calming motion for a couple minutes, yes, but really, it's just giving my kids some good old fashioned stories about how nuts their mom was when they were little. What if my kids are spared the 'payback offspring' and never need to turn into *Mommy Dearest*?

I guess what my folks were saying is that spanking hurts parents more emotionally than physically. I'm apparently still learning the hard way. It is so challenging to discipline your children. You want what's best for them, but being their friend is not an option. I suppose if I'm doing an okay job as a parent, we can be friends once they reach the ripe old age of twenty. That is if they're not in therapy telling all their good *Mommy Dearest* stories.

So, moral of the story, I spank my kids. When that doesn't work, I double spank my kids. I'm still figuring this whole thing out, but I guarantee that the love I have for them far outweighs my 'I'll Never'. It's Okay.

Homework Hoopla

I'll never ... do my child's homework!

Well, my 'I'll Never' is hard to admit, but I have to be honest; we were just flat out overwhelmed with life. After settling into life with three children, my husband and I found that we were both deprived of time; time to just get life accomplished and it was our oldest son's first year of school. I mean who would have thought that we'd be dealing with homework in kindergarten? Each week my son brought home little books that he was supposed to practice reading to us. We had a calendar for each month and my son was supposed to color a box for each day he read to us.

Finding time to sit down and read with our five-year-old son should have been our top priority. I mean he is the next generation that will be taking care of this fine world we live in. Plus taking care of me one day when I am old and gray. Anyway, finding time was difficult. We would still frequently sit down with all three children and read to them, but the two youngest children were so distracting that it became more and more challenging for him to read to us. He was still at the stage that every word took close to 30 seconds to figure out and reading a whole book could take an hour with the other two interrupting.

One month we had done so poorly that I was ashamed and embarrassed. I couldn't imagine sending in a blank calendar. I mean, what would this teacher think? We are good parents. We want our children to succeed. My guilt got the best of me and before sending back the sheet to school, I colored in a few boxes to make it look like he had read more. My son had no idea I did this, but really, who does their kids' homework? I guess I do.

While this was not my proudest parenting moment, it's our crazy life raising multiple children in multiple stages of development all with multiple needs. I've realized sometimes we just need to survive and that year we did, though one month short of *really* doing reading homework. It's Okay.

Food Fanatics

I'll never ... let my kid eat fast food; at least not before the age of four!

I'll admit it. I used to think horribly of people who would let their children eat greasy cheeseburgers. I would see babies in McDonald's eating the unhealthiest food available. These parents seemed oblivious to the fact that they were single-handedly destroying their child's diet. I vowed then and there, NEVER to let my child eat fast food (at least until he or she was four ... thinking by then I would have filled him or her up with enough goodness that one cheeseburger wouldn't do irreparable damage). I know, my thinking may have been a little skewed, but I was pregnant and bound and determined to raise the perfect child.

Fast forward to two years later; my one-and-a-half-year-old was throwing the tantrum of his life in the backseat of the car. I had held true to my 'I'll Never'. Even if my hubby and I were eating out, our little guy would not get to touch an ounce of the grease. So, back to the tantrum—I handed my wallet back in hopes of keeping him quiet just long enough for me to get through ordering my food. Yes, I was heading into the drive-thru of a fast food restaurant. Hey, no judging; I never admitted to being perfect. Besides, the food was only for me, of course, not my son.

Well, as I was finishing up my order and putting the car into drive, I felt an object hit the back of my head rather abruptly. I looked down to the object that had fallen near my feet; it was my credit card. I, of course, had pulled out the needed cash to pay for my quick meal, but why did he chuck my card at me? Not two seconds later, my boy, in his best language possible, was shouting, "ME WANT CHEESEBURGER NOW!" He repeated these words over and over again. Then I felt another prick in the back of the head. Repeat of the card action. What the heck? He was throwing my credit cards at me, one by one, so that I would buy him a cheeseburger.

As all good mothers do, I caved. I did my 'I'll Never'. I bought my boy his cheeseburger that day and he has had too many to count since then. I try to make myself feel better by overloading him with fruits and veggies, but I sometimes fail at that, too. My preconceived notions about feeding my kids fast food had to change. It's too easy, it's too convenient and it creates too much quiet for us not to indulge occasionally! I lived and learned! And ... my kids eat fast food. It's Okay.

Bedtime Slip-Up

I'll never ... put my baby to bed with a bottle!

Sometime, somewhere, I heard or read that if I gave my baby a bottle lying down or while in bed, that his/her teeth would rot and fall out. Whenever I saw a baby lying on the floor with a bottle, or saw a friend sending a kid off to bed with a bottle, I would secretly vow never to be that desperate. I would never allow my baby a feeding time without love and cuddling or create an opportunity to rot my child's teeth. Ha! Guess I should have never said, "I'll Never."

With my first two children, I can honestly say that I never let them have a bottle on their back, in bed or without someone holding them. After all, this was supposed to be their 'connecting' time, right? Of course, I would have rather been nursing them until they no longer needed a bottle, but somehow I was blessed with 'skim' breast milk that didn't keep them growing at the proper rate after a certain point (that's another story that included eating oatmeal, taking an obscene amount of herbal pills and pumping my boobs flaccid) and I had to resort to formula. So bottle feeding was a regular occurrence at our house.

Anyway, child number three came around and I had very little patience at bedtime after dealing with my older two children. I somehow convinced myself that putting a baby to bed with a bottle every once in a while wasn't the end of the world. I mean, people nurse in the middle of the night all the time. These kids fall asleep on the boob and I'm sure their mothers don't wipe their mouths out after every feeding or take a tooth brush to their teeth. How could this be any different? For a moment, images of my child with black teeth and/or missing teeth crept into my head. But, serious sleep deprivation swiftly erased them and I finally caved. It wasn't every night, or all the time, but I did it. I failed.

I did my 'I'll Never'. My baby went to bed with a bottle. Boy, were those nights peaceful. Please don't take this as permission to do my failed parenting, but know there is always a silver lining. My third child still has all her teeth and not one of them is black. It's Okay.

Triumphant Toilet

I'll never ... let my kid play in the toilet!

Seriously, what kind of parents let their kid play in the toilet? I mean do these people even watch their children? How unsafe, unhealthy and just down right disgusting. Do these parents not know how to teach their children right from wrong? I knew before I had children, that my kid would never have a Barbie in the toilet, dip a washcloth in the toilet, or wash off his toothbrush in the toilet. I knew this would never, never happen.

Well, it was a sad day in my parenting world when I had child number two. While he was a blessing, he tested me and all my parenting standards. It seemed that my quality parenting went to pot and got left by the side of the road. That second child of mine was not at all like my first. I don't think I had to safety lock one thing with my first child. No outlets needed covering, no kid safety locks were needed on drawers or cupboards; the child just didn't get into stuff. I watched her like a hawk and was sure to raise the perfect child, starting time-outs at the age of nine months. I had this parenting thing figured out and didn't really understand how parents could be so lazy to not keep their kids out of disgusting places like the toilet.

Oops! I should have never said those two dreaded words. That second child of mine and later my third child put my parenting skills to shame. I had too many ah-ha moments to count as my second child neared his first birthday. Cell phones were dropped in cups of water, pacifiers were played with in the toilets and toys were stuck

It's Okay

in the outlets. I couldn't even turn around without him getting into something. I couldn't move harmful things out of the way fast enough. Heck, he found things I didn't even know were dangerous. The toilet became the least of my concerns. Note to new parents or those moving to new houses—lever door handles are not the answer. No room is safe or out of reach of those naughty little people we call children. Those darn handles can be turned from the age of one.

Oh well, my kids are all still alive and now using the toilet to actually go to the bathroom, rather than just for a pool of water to splash in. I admit it; my kid DID play in the toilet. It's Okay.

Highchair Horror

I'll never ... have a highchair in my house as disgusting as that one!

There were many friends of mine who had young children before I became a mother. I knew that my parenting skills would far surpass them all and I had a few pointers I would have liked to share, given the opportunity (these pointers ranged from snotty nosed kids to mismatched ensembles to bratty behavior). The thing that bothered me most, that I seemed to encounter often, was dirty highchairs. I mean maybe my friends needed their eyes checked or needed to understand how bacteria grows. This could have been a quick science lesson I'd have been happy to give. The grime and disgusting look of most high chairs was about enough for me to buy them an extra tube of Clorox wipes. Or a new high chair. Some were so bad, they might as well have started over. How long had it been since these people actually took a washcloth to the high chair? My thoughts were, "Seriously, just wait until I have children."

I swore many times that I would NEVER have dirty high chairs like the ones I had experienced 'pre' children. Oh, how I wish I would have known. I wish I would have known that each meal brings a week's worth of cleaning to a chair and a floor. Those parents who had dogs may have had the cleanest kitchens, aside from the dog hair. Each meal is like a warzone and the chair becomes the unfortunate target. Now having children that I go to war with each meal, I realize that I may have spoken or thought unrealistic expectations. Instead of, "I'll never have disgusting high chairs," it's more like, "Geez, I hope I hide my dirt better than my friends used to!"

So, I guess now I'm the one who could use a short 101 in Science. My high chairs get dirty, too, and many of the other things I said I'd never do have been done as well. I didn't realize all the battles I'd have to fight as a parent and I now know that I certainly can't fight them all. It's Okay.

Couch Potato

I'll never ... let my kid watch too much television!

TV will rot your child's brain. Can you believe that people actually use TV as a babysitter? All the research out there shows how detrimental TV can be and that children under the age of three shouldn't even have the TV on while they are in a room playing. We all want our kids to be the best they can be, so why would anyone do something as harmful as letting their child watch TV? Unfortunately, those were the questions I would have asked BEFORE I had children, BEFORE I realized the answers.

Why? I'll tell you why. Kids are crazy. Parents need a break. Parents need to cook dinner. Parents need to stay sane. Parents sometimes need to do a load of laundry, clean a toilet or for goodness sakes, need to read a chapter in a parenting book. These researchers and authors that know what is 'best' for kids could not have been parents themselves. Because if they were, my 'I'll Never' wouldn't have happened.

We were really strict for a while with the TV rule. Trying to limit it as much as possible and making movies a really big deal. That started our Friday Family Movie Night. The whole family would snuggle up and watch a movie together eating popcorn and enjoying each other's company. Well, as time went on, the 'family' night got changed into 'kids' night. We no longer snuggled in, but rather used those two hours of peace to clean up from our week, do some bills, or even just enjoy a beer and chat about our weekly happenings. It'd be nice to say that was the only time our babysitter was free, but TV has kept us sane and kept our house manageable.

So TV is not a never in our house—our TV babysitter costs as much as our Red Box video and we once again had to eat our words (this has happened more times than we can count). It's Okay.

Sleeping Mate

I'll never ... co-sleep with my child!

Does it count if I only did it during the day? I had said I'd never co-sleep with my baby; won't happen, no exceptions, no way, no how. I mean, technically, I kept my 'I'll Never,' because I never co-slept with my baby during the night. Who would have thought my newborn wouldn't have been the most pleasant child I could have asked for? Who would have thought that my level of exhaustion I felt during the first few months of her life would be so overwhelming that I would do ANYTHING to get some sleep?

I didn't want to lose all my principals so I found creative ways to co-sleep. I had convinced myself that day hours did not count. I just had her lay on my chest while I was lying on the couch. Let's be honest, the TV was on, so how could this possibly have counted as co-sleeping? There were also those times that I would bring her into bed to nurse in the early hours of the morning where she would occasionally (or daily ... who's counting?), fall asleep. Technically we had started a new day and those few hours she slept in my bed weren't really part of the night-time sleeping, right? I mean all the books say that you shouldn't wake a sleeping baby and the books know best.

So, as I look back, I may have had to eat my 'I'll Never' words. I suppose my co-sleeping happened if we get technical. My principles are still strong, I've just learned not to voice them as loud in case they need to adapt and change as my parenting world constantly turns. It's Okay.

Criminal Activity

I'll never ... let my kids play violent games!

"Violent games lead to violent people. We will not have guns in our house, even if they are for pretend. There are too many crimes these days and children hurting other children." Those were my famous words, unsupported by my husband who grew up with guns for hunting, before we had children. While these were my words and my principles, I was sure they were strong enough for both me and my husband. When I say I was sure, I guess deep down I knew what he really believed and that his words would be, "What's it going to hurt, he's a boy?" Because I knew this, it was a pleasant surprise that our first child was a girl. It became an issue we could put high up on the shelf and deal with at a time far and away.

Unfortunately my principles were tested when my second child was born. He was a boy. We didn't find out what we were having before the birth, but I knew it was a girl. I had that 'motherly' feeling. I carried like a girl, I felt the same as I did with my first baby girl and my instinct told me, girl. So, when the baby was pulled out and the doctor said, "It's a boy," my reaction was one to write home about. "Oh, shit!" It might be important to add that there were over ten people in the delivery room. I probably shouldn't admit to this, but I was really nervous. I was not prepared to handle a boy. Especially if he turned out like my sarcastic hubby, whom I love dearly, but who I have heard was a challenging child and is *still* a slightly challenging adult.

My son was born. He spent many years content playing with his sister's toys and dressing up in his sister's dresses. He even liked getting his nails painted. But, he was different. He was wild. He was starting to turn every toy into a weapon. Flashes of criminal activity and jail time haunted my thoughts for him in the future.

I tried so hard not to give in. My principles were strong. Not! My dad once said, "We played cops and robbers all the time when I was growing up and we all turned out fine!" I suppose he is right. There were far fewer crimes when he was young (or at least little media to make the crimes known to the public). And so, I lost the battle. We now have many, many guns and even more weapons. Paint sticks are the sword of choice and sadly, there is a wooden cross that serves as a knife in some games. Not only did I lose the battle, but apparently all my principles as well.

I still speak to my children about violence and encourage kind-loving princess games. But, hey, even every princess story has a prince that has to battle evil. It's Okay.

Picture Perfect

I'll never ... be one of those parents that take a picture every two minutes!

Seriously, those parents that carry a camera around their neck at all times are ridiculous, right? Well, that is what I thought until I became one of them. Before I had children, I'd get updates from my friends every week with pictures posted of their children in the highchair, on the potty, sitting on the step. Just these everyday things that I swore I would never succumb to. I didn't understand why I needed to see ten shots of the kid doing the same thing over and over. I mean there may have been a slight change in their smile, but really? Cute? Sure, they were, I guess. Obsessive parent? Must be, yes, definitely!

Well, I should have never had those thoughts until I understood how precious those smiles were. There isn't enough wall space to house all the photos of my two children. And thank goodness for technology where I can store THOUSANDS of pictures and videos. Love, love, love the photo websites. My children are both under the age of two. What is to come of me? My husband tries to draw the line with the professional photography. He is somewhat frugal and tries to remind me of my old ways of thinking. Oops, too late. I can't imagine not having a photo of each special smirk, grin or wide-open mouth smile.

Videos are another downfall of mine. My husband and I used to think that America's Funniest Home Videos was the dumbest show we had ever seen. If it happened to pop up when we were flipping channels, we would roll our eyes as if to say, "We will never be those kinds of parents to record every moment of our children's lives." I mean why did parents think these videos were even interesting? Why on earth did they have their video camera out when all their kid was doing was sitting in the high chair, with a mixture of drool and cut up banana on his cheek? Clearly the kid did not know how to hold a spoon or find his mouth. Most of the time, the kid couldn't even talk back to the parent and the parent sounded ridiculous making high pitch noises to which the kid only created a more disgusting mixture of food and spit.

Well, again, we spoke too soon. We are those people. We love it. It's precious to look back at old videos and laugh. I get it now, I so get it. I have to dump photos and videos off my camera almost weekly because it gets too full (mostly full of those ridiculous 20 second videos I once hated watching). I now also get to be the one who sends out the photos and videos on a regular basis. Well, okay, daily. I sometimes wonder if my family and friends think of me the way my hubby and I used to think of America's Funniest Home Videos.

Oh well, it's okay. My kids are worth every photo and video I've taken, plus a million things more. I broke my 'I'll Never'. I'm already over it. It's Okay.

CHAPTER II

'Til Death Do Us Part ... At Least Before We Had Kids

Marriage is such a joyful thing. It's always tranquil, relaxed, enjoyable and full of caring, kind, compassionate words. Ha! Go ahead and laugh now. Any couple that has encountered the sacrament of marriage for longer than a year knows that it can be wonderful, but it can also be very infuriating. Not just infuriating, but down right maddening, annoying, exasperating and irritating. The most challenging part of marriage comes from trying to communicate with this person that is supposed to be your other half. If he is truly my other half, then why when we sync our phone calendars do I still wonder if he is smart enough to look at it? Why do I have to ask for help folding clothes? What the heck does my other half think I'm going to do with this basket full of clean clothes ... pile it up so the kids can jump in it like leaves? Get off your butt and help fold already.

We can all agree marriage is hard. Adding a new bundle of joy into these two halves becomes a new torturous adventure. This adventure is not one that any marriage can fully prepare for. What will this new little person do to our 50/50 agreement? How will we equally share this experience? Of course, before this new little person comes into the world, the couple is in agreement about how each of them will contribute and how much added love they will have for each other because they are going raise this new little person together. Seriously? More love for one another? Obviously no one wants to get 'real' about having a newborn. No one talks about how a new baby will create crabby, sleep-deprived, sex-deprived, bitter people that are supposed to love one another until death do them part.

Pregnancy is the first little insight into how a baby will change a marriage. This skips over the steps of becoming pregnant, which can be a whole added stressor into how two people communicate their love for one another. Or become robots at ovulation time to 'make' a baby out of love. And what about those couples who struggle to get pregnant or who have to wait months or years for adoption? The anticipation wears on a marriage and the spunk that the marriage once had. The baby isn't even home yet and already the marriage is strained.

So, being pregnant is ABSOLUTELY amazing, right? What if I said, no? If we get 'real' about this thing we call parenting, we have to get 'real' about this thing that people call a 'miracle' or a 'bun in the oven'. Now people will say that they loved being pregnant. Are they being honest? Or are they just forgetting all the horrible parts that come with pregnancy? Getting fat, being bloated, snoring, being gassy, having to pee every 20 minutes, peeing yourself, not fitting in normal chairs, having an uncontrollable outbreak of back-acne, wearing clothes that are NOT comfortable or wearing comfortable clothes and looking like a tent—the list is endless. Spouses now have to deal with a woman that is not the woman they married. These pregnant women don't look or smell like the ones they married, and they certainly don't ACT like the women they married either. P.S. They're crazy!

Pregnancy leads to a beautiful and precious gift, but there is a lot of crap that people choose not to talk about because it makes them sound like they don't appreciate the fact that they are pregnant; or like they are taking for granted this amazing opportunity to bring a life into the world. Pregnancy does some crazy things to people, but in the end, when the precious gift finally arrives, it's okay that there may have been some negative thoughts or feelings. It truly is worth every struggle and every change.

Remember, it's okay if your marriage struggles along with the adjustments of children. It's okay that your marriage may never be the same. It's okay to not like your spouse some days. It's okay to need some time apart, to work hard to stay connected as a couple, to spend time together away from your kids, to find creative ways to stay intimate, to learn to like each other for new reasons. It's all part of struggling as a married couple with children. It's okay.

Dorito Doosie

Let me start from the beginning. Nacho Cheese Doritos were my favorite thing to eat when I was pregnant. Well, okay, every food bad for me was my favorite thing to eat when I was pregnant. That's not the point. We had tacos the night before this incident and there were only a few chips left in the bag. These few chips were all I could think about that day at work. I knew when I got home from a long day at work that I would have limited time to eat and get ready for a night of sand volleyball. I was beyond excited to unroll that bag of chips, tilt it up to my mouth and let those last few chips roll into my mouth. Oh the crumbs. I knew I would have to raise the bag at least two or three times. It was the highlight of my day just imaging the taste of those darn chips.

Now, maybe I had overdone myself. I was so tired and wasn't looking forward to driving all the way across town to play volleyball after a long day at work. I was hopeful the chips would spark my energy. That is when the tears began; not just tears, but a blubbering waterfall. I walked into our kitchen after changing my clothes for volleyball (which I only had one pair of shorts that didn't really fit and was already upset about having to wear them), ready to down the only thing that would help my dampened mood … my chips! There, in the corner of our kitchen, stood my husband; my uncaring, unsympathetic, un-pregnant husband. That jerk had those chips sliding down his own rotten throat. Every last delicious crumb—GONE!

I thought I might die. It was the breaking point. I couldn't even look at him. I tried to regain my composure the whole way to volleyball, hoping that my swollen belly would overshadow my swollen eyes. I mean what would I say? "He ate my chips." Technically they weren't even my chips, BUT, *they were*. I was the one who was pregnant. I was the one who was dealing with my changing body and changing moods. That jerk! What was he thinking? It's Okay.

Pancake Throw

What is it with our unchanging minds when we are pregnant? The entire week, all I wanted to do was eat pancakes on Saturday morning. I couldn't settle for the box mix, oh no. I was going to have fresh pancakes made from scratch; I was going to be fancy. As a new mom, I was going to be fancy and make things from scratch. It all was going to start that dreadful Saturday morning. I was so excited that I couldn't make just one batch, I needed a double batch. My mouth was watering just thinking about how good those amazing pancakes were going to be.

Something went wrong. Wrong, wrong, wrong. They tasted all wrong. To make matters worse, my husband tried to tell me they tasted fine—fine? What the hell did he know? There I was having a 'fine' pregnancy, with very few mood swings and no complications. Who the hell did he think he was telling me those pancakes tasted fine? I didn't want 'fine,' I wanted 'mouth-watering'.

So, as any reasonable person would do, I decided to throw the pancakes one by one across the kitchen at the oven. Why would I start over or just add extra butter and syrup to make them taste better? Why wouldn't I just act rationally and take my loving husband out for pancakes. Well, I'll tell you why. These things doctors call hormones is why. They got the best of me that Saturday morning and my dog got the best of my pancakes. It's Okay.

Cheater

The Fourth of July left me overly hot and peeing way too much. These facts didn't sit well with me since I had sat in a hot tub recently and over-indulged in alcoholic beverages on numerous occasions in the four weeks prior. I was pregnant and expecting my very first child. I was thrilled (minus the guilt I felt about all my previous un-pregnant like activities) and felt extremely blessed. At this point in the pregnancy, I was unaware that this little bean was going to be a spirited girl who would play tricks on my hormones and bring out my inner craze that is apparently hidden deep inside.

So imagine me, a newly pregnant woman, doing laundry and finding a house key in my husband's pocket. Mind you, this was not *our* house key. Who wouldn't assume that the lying, cheating bastard took his first opportunity to find a fresh piece of meat instead of wanting this pregnant body now overtaking his wife? Jerk (this isn't the word I would have chosen, but the others aren't appropriate for this book)! Here we were, having our first baby, starting this new journey together and he was cheating on me.

I had to confront him. Thoughts of single parenthood overwhelmed me. How was this going to work? I'd get the house; screw him and his dog. I never wanted that dog anyway. I stood my ground firm, shoving the key in his face and asking him whose it was. His bewildered look was almost believable. He stood there, lying through his cheating teeth, saying he had no idea where the key came from. He used the excuse that he'd been with me for the past week non-stop. Of course he had, until I passed out dead to the world at night because I was so exhausted. That was probably when all this funny business was occurring.

The confrontation did not go well. I fumed. I ranted. Was I not attractive enough anymore? Was I getting too flabby for him to love? I mean what was going to happen when I was actually showing? He continued to look at me with this puzzled, again almost believable, look and swore he had no idea what I was talking about. He ended up in his man cave and I didn't talk to him for days. Jerk.

That's when the pregnancy brain took a brief break and let my old self back into the picture. I started recalling him cleaning out the junk drawer a few days prior and briefly remember him mumbling something about old keys. Oh no. Oh, no, no, no. I looked at the key again. Oh no. It couldn't be. It was. Not only was my husband not cheating on me, but the key he had in his pocket was an old babysitting key that

I had used in college. I was freaking crazy. Was this what people call 'prego-brain'? Thank goodness I have a loving husband who is still willing to be wed to me until death do us part. It's Okay.

Poor Parked Car

What was my husband thinking? There I was 36-weeks pregnant with our fourth child and he was going fishing. Yes, fishing. He was leaving me working full-time, caring for our three crazy children and trying to deal with the fact that we would be having a baby any day. Well, so the chances of having the baby any day were slim; we'd had three previous C-section deliveries and the chance of a 'normal' or early birth was out of the question, but I'm digressing from the real issue. My husband was the issue. Of course, I encouraged him to go, but by that point in our marriage, shouldn't he have been able to read through the lines? Shouldn't he have known that I really didn't *want* him to go?

So he went. He left me. Not only did he leave me, but he left me with his horrendous pile of metal that he called a car. I don't need to mention that this was technically *my* old car. Again, that was not the issue. He was the issue. So I was driving his four door hunk of junk. I could barely get buckled in. I couldn't see two feet past the front of the car because my belly was so big and I couldn't get the broken seat to go up.

I left work briefly, hopeful that a #2 from McDonalds and an extra-large coke (yes, I drank caffeine ... it was my fourth child) would brighten my mood. Of course, I immediately started eating those delicious fries on the short drive back to work. Entering the parking lot, licking my greasy fingers, I looked for a place to park. Perfect. It was my day. Right up front, second stall, open! I cranked the wheel, excited to enjoy my grease and kept right on driving. Fast forward to my head jerking forward, a horrible crunching noise (not from my fries) and my car coming to a complete stop.

Oh, could that day have gotten any worse? I hit a car. A parked car! Who hits a parked car? I was feeling fine besides the agonizing emotions of embarrassment and horror. How was I going to approach this co-worker? "Gee, sorry I rammed into your parked car." Suddenly my food didn't seem so appetizing. I dropped the food in my office and headed toward my co-worker. She was unbelievably kind. I'm sure she felt sorry for me and my over-sized body. I was teary-eyed and choked up. The damage was minimal, but I still offered to pay for any re-painting necessary.

Well, I hit a parked car. There are a million excuses I could rattle off as to why it happened, but there is really only one that mattered. My husband; it was entirely his fault! It's Okay.

Sticky Note Nonsense

When I was pregnant with my second child, our oldest was just over one. Needless to say, I didn't have time to put my feet up or prepare in the way I had with my first child. Throughout the pregnancy I was bound and determined to fix, organize and clean EVERYTHING in the house. It was going to be perfect. I had plenty of time and it was going to be done, done, and more done before that baby came home from the hospital.

People talk about a nesting period; well mine was a nesting pregnancy. I had heard that with two kids it'd be difficult to get things done. No problem on this end, I was going to have it all done before the baby even arrived. I began going through every room in the house, picking apart every nook and cranny, every closet; there was not a spot in the house that would be untouched and perfect. In order to keep my memory sharp of everything I wanted to do, sticky notes became my new best friend.

Sticky notes were plastered in every room, on every closet door and all across our coffee table and desk. These dear notes contained not just an item or two on each, but lists of things to disinfect, go through, clean or organize. I went through pads of sticky notes and I have to say, I was delighted at my determination. My husband, however, did not find the same joy as I did from these little squares now covering our house.

With a one-year-old running around and my pregnant body growing more tired by the day, many of the sticky notes still remained. My husband grew to despise my lists and my sticky notes. Our desk and table still covered (we lived like this for months) and lists not getting crossed off as fast as I hoped, baby number two arrived with many things still to finish. While many of the items remained unorganized or corners not completely sanitized, I had put forth my best effort. One thing is for sure, you can't blame a mom for trying and you certainly can't talk sanity with a pregnant lady. It's Okay.

Labor-less

I was a first time pregnant gal, awaiting the arrival of my new bundle. It was six weeks away, so there was no need to panic or over-prepare. Birthing class was right around the corner and surely after that, we would have all the needed information. My husband had planned his last night out with friends and as I shipped him out the door, I had no idea what was in store for me.

I should rewind to earlier in the week. It was about Wednesday or so and I was visiting with a college friend on the phone. She was asking about how things were going. I informed her that things were good, but I was having some back pain and some spotting. I knew I had a doctor's appointment the next week and assured her that I would follow up with these minor concerns. At the time I thought she was crazy. She started saying things like, "You know, those are signs of labor," and, "Has your doctor checked you yet?" I brushed off her comments knowing that surely if I was going to have this baby early, I, of all people, would know!

Back to Friday evening and my husband heading out the door to enjoy his last night out before becoming a father. I truly was excited for him and although I was having an eye issue, I told him to go have fun. This eye issue turned into more than I could have ever bargained for. My sister came over that evening to watch a movie with me and made a big deal out of my eye. Again, like with my friend on the phone, I thought she was overreacting. She insisted we go in to get it checked out.

After she forced me out the door and drove me to the doctor, I was having doubts about going in. I'm not one to waste money and this didn't seem to be that pressing. But, once the doctor saw me, it turned out that my sister had good cause to bring me in. It was a scratched cornea. While I was there, they wanted to get me on a monitor to check in on the baby. All I could think about was that I hated all the fuss and I just wanted to go home to enjoy the movie.

The nurse came in after I was on the monitor and asked me how I was feeling. Seriously, they wouldn't leave me alone. She mentioned that the monitor showed that I was having regular contractions very close together and looked at me very concerned-like. "Let's just check you out!" Oh my goodness. Enough already; I just wanted to go home. "Well, you're not going to be able to go home." She then announced with a smile, "You're going to have a baby tonight!"

WHAT? WHAT? A BABY! No, no, no. I went in for a scratched cornea, not to have a baby. There was a lot of hustle and bustle for a few moments and then I remember them calling my husband. I had put off the inevitable, wanting him to have an enjoyable evening out with friends. A short time later, my drunken (very drunken) husband stumbled into the hospital. Several cups of coffee later, he became aware that he was soon to become a father. My joy for his last night out had turned into hatred for the awful smell that had occupied the entire room … probably the entire maternity ward.

We delivered our first baby boy the next morning. It was not at all like I had expected, turns out most deliveries aren't! We never made it to birthing class that weekend; I guess it wouldn't have helped much at that point anyway. And, I had to call my friend and inform her that she may have been right about me being in labor. I never knew! My eye saved the day. We still look back at the pictures of me, my eye patch and my new bundle of joy, and laugh. And, I'm still surprised that the hospital trusted my drunken husband (who in his poor state also asked

for some nitroglycerin) enough to actually send us home with a baby!
It's Okay.

Potato Soup Sadness

My ever-so-patient husband lost his tolerance for me one pregnant evening. After slaving away in the kitchen all afternoon baking
five batches of Christmas cut-out cookies, I was starving. While I was
doing a kind and sweet gesture for our friends and neighbors, I couldn't
wait another moment to eat dinner. The only problem was that nothing sounded good. Decisions were apparently not my strong suit at
the time, but who can blame a hungry pregnant gal? My husband got
home from work and tried his hardest to help me figure out what dinner options we had. He rattled off all the foods that had been staple
pregnancy items (egg rolls were at the top of the list). Nothing sounded
good. As he continued to throw out suggestions, my irritation and star-
vation continued to increase.

As a last ditch effort, we decided to get in the car and drive around
until we found something that sounded good. Finally, we passed
Panera Bread. Wednesday was Potato Soup Day! Potato soup sounded
PERFECT! I could see the relief sweep over my husband now that the
dinner dilemma had been solved.

As we walked in to Panera Bread, I almost had a skip in my step. So
hungry and so excited to eat. We walked up to order from an overly-
chipper teenaged server. "Two potato soup bread bowls, please!" Our
order was short and sweet and I knew the soup would be out in no time
at all.

I did not like our server's smiley response one bit. "Oh, like, the
weirdest thing happened today. Some big company, like, came in
and ordered, like, all the potato soup for their lunches. So, like, we're
totally out. This, like, never happens." She went on and on, all annoy-
ingly upbeat, continuing to explain why the restaurant was out of the
only freaking thing that sounded good to me and she was completely
oblivious to how absolutely miserable she was making me. I tuned her
out entirely as all my hopes for eating dinner came crashing down.

My husband looked down at me and me up at him with tears prick-
ling in my eyes. He said in the most loving way possible, "I don't think

I can handle it if you cry right now." My reply was not quite as loving. "Then I think we should leave."

I barely got to the car before I broke down in tears. We drove home. I got out, dumped all the Christmas cookies in a garbage bag and threw them into the snow-covered yard. That night I went to bed without dinner. I am not exactly sure what the cookies did wrong or what my husband decided on for dinner. One thing is for sure, I had a big breakfast the next morning and a fresh start was exactly what I needed. It's Okay.

Lies

When we found out we were pregnant with our first child, we were so elated. We survived the moods of pregnancy, the ever changing body parts and even the ridiculous farts, snores, stuffy noses and burps. I have to admit that I got tired of hearing his ridiculous comments. "Well, now you know what it's like to be me!" Or, "Welcome to my world!" Oh, my husband, the joker. So supportive, but really, he had all those issues because he was a gross, disgusting male, not because he was a storage facility and cafeteria for our unborn child. It was MY time to be self-centered and his time to be sympathetic!

Besides the comments, he really was supportive and the support continued well into the birth of our first child. For the first few weeks, he was a real trooper. Up in the middle of the night with every feeding, changing diapers, listening to concerns—really amazing. I had no idea what I was going to complain to my friends about. He was remarkable.

Oops, spoke too soon. I realized, rather abruptly, that I would have plenty to complain about. The third week of life hit hard for our first child and all of a sudden my husband was deaf, dumb and incompetent. Why would he have the answers? He wondered why I would call my friends to ask their advice; well, I will tell you why. Any time I wanted to brainstorm or problem solve to figure that little person out, all he would say was, "How the hell am I supposed to know?"

We laugh about these things now, surviving our children and the changes our marriage has encountered. But ... there are still many moments when the deafness, dumbness and incompetence set in. This leads me to the lying. I had to have some way to get rest and sleeping in was my only chance. Being up all night and functioning during the day was more than unbearable. When you multiply this day after day and year after year, I was practically a walking zombie. So, maybe my little one didn't really get up every hour last night. Or maybe I wasn't up four times like I said. Or maybe I really only got up one time to put in a pacifier. After years of doing the nights while he snored like a grizzly bear, I deserved a little sleep.

Boy, were those mornings nice. I could usually buy myself at least an extra hour. It was just a little white lie and I was so much better for it. Hey, it's okay, right? At least as long as he doesn't figure out this story is about him. It's Okay.

Left Alone

Pregnancy and children do some strange things to the relationship you have with your spouse. Not that being married is easy without these two things, but the strains that they create cannot be prepared for. You'd think that after three pregnancies and three flourishing children, a fourth pregnancy couldn't do that much more damage to a relationship. Boy was I wrong.

My fourth pregnancy was going along without any complications and life was continuing at a fast pace. Our three children were driving us crazy as ever, but everyone was healthy and functioning (well, the kids were at least). I was a pregnant mommy working full time, trying to balance home and work, trying to stay healthy (to not indulge in too much caffeine or fast food) and then trying to be a good wife. Something had to give and my job of 'wife' went by the wayside.

So imagine a small squabble about parenting differences. Kids have a tendency to take advantage of situations and ours were certainly capitalizing on their mother being worn down. Papa bear picked up their new strategy of wearing mama bear down so much until she caved. He became fed up with their behavior and put down the big boom; the big roar. Sensitive mama bear felt sorry for her naughty little cubs and let emotions take over. She roared at papa bear and didn't back him up (big blunder in the marriage world). This started a brawl like no other.

Words were shared; insensitive comments screamed. The children just stood by, not sure what to do with this new reaction from their mother. All sorts of thoughts streamed through my hormone-filled brain; thoughts from how we ended up with three kids to why on earth we would decide to bring another one into this 'bear-like' family. I'd had enough and didn't know what else to do. I did what all sensible people would do (not!) and I announced, "I'm leaving."

I walked down the steps, grabbed my keys and waddled myself out to squeeze into the car. I drove out the driveway, down the street and around the block. This three minute drive was enough for me to realize that I was overreacting and that I really had no place to go. I parked the car, walked back in house, hung up the keys and was greeted by my husband. The greeting was one that I hadn't expected. He busted out laughing. He was almost crying he was laughing so hard. "Where'd you go? You weren't gone very long! Did you have a nice drive?" I couldn't help myself but join in. The kids came down to us giggling and hugging. It's Okay.

Cravings

Staying at home with my two beautiful girls had not gone without its sacrifices. I was an avid shopper before staying at home, not needing a reason to buy a new pair of shoes. My shopping days had come to a halt and I became extremely resourceful in order to maintain my stay-at-home status. Becoming pregnant with my third child put my thriftiness to the test. Eating out was ALL I wanted to do.

My girls at home didn't need much to fill their bellies, so I was still able to get my fast food 'fix' while only spending a few dollars. Funny thing is, I'm a phenomenal cook and I love to bake in the kitchen. The problem was that NOTHING I could cook sounded as good as the greasy fast food I could purchase. So the day that I realized I had a two for the price of one coupon at Qdoba Mexican Grill, I couldn't get my brain hooked on anything but a wrap!

Being the kind and considerate wife that I am, I called my husband to see if he wanted to do lunch. He takes his work very seriously and is quite possibly the hardest worker I know. Leaving for lunch is not an option for him. So I tried to please and offered to bring lunch to him.

He could just run out to the car, grab this cheap lunch and not miss any work time. Perfect!

I was out and about running errands with the kids and lunchtime couldn't come fast enough. Well, it was at that moment, I realized that my two for one coupon was tied up in my e-mail, which was on my computer, AT MY HOUSE. I didn't know at that time how my lunchtime fantasy would turn into a flurry of small nightmares. Since I was already out and about, it would have been fabulous to be able to pull up my e-mail on my phone. Ha! Did I mention that staying at home had its sacrifices? One of the sacrifices we had made was that we were still living in the 18th century with phones that didn't have internet access.

I found a payphone, pulled over, looked in a phone book (yes, these still exist—I don't know why I didn't just call 411) and called the restaurant to find out if I needed the coupon in hand to get the discount. The answer was, of course, yes. What to do? I could have just given up and gone home, forgetting about my lunch. But, with hormones flaring, that would have been too easy. The library wasn't too far away, so I made a pit stop.

I unbuckled the two girls and carted them into the local library. "Do you have an open computer with internet access I could use?" My heart was sinking, but they had an open computer. Perfect! "Can I print?" Please, oh please, I was pleading. I could print for ten cents. Great! "Do you take a check card?" Of course, all my change was in the car and all I had was a credit card on me. "Sorry, we don't accept credit cards."

I went *back* out to the car, two girls in hand, grabbed my change and headed back into the local library. I handed over the ten cents, got on the computer, pulled up my e-mail and printed the coupon. Out we went AGAIN. I buckled in the two girls and headed off to enjoy my delicious wrap. Everything was working out. I ordered the two wraps and started enjoying my lunch, thinking the girls would want nothing to do with my wrap. Wrong AGAIN!

By the time I got to my husband's work, I had only gotten to indulge in a fourth of my wrap. I begrudgingly handed over his lunch to him and mentioned that I didn't even get to eat my whole wrap. He unsympathetically asked, "Well, do you want half of mine?" Maybe if there was some sincerity or some gratitude in his voice, I might have accepted. But, my spirits had been so dampened by the morning fiasco that I instead just went home to pout. It's Okay.

CHAPTER III

But, The Book Said ...

Weve all been there; been struggling at one point or another in our parenting journey. It's at those times that we call a good friend, call the doctor or consult the all-knowing parenting books. There's a book out there for every problem under the sun. Every problem, that is, except the one that is exactly like the one you seem to be having. Once you finally consult the books and try everything suggested, you realize that it's really not about what the books say, but about your own situation. What works for your friend, the doctor or for the author of the book you're reading, may not work for you.

In trying to figure out how to fix the problem you are having, inevitably another problem arises. So now the original problem isn't really the problem anymore and there are three other things needing to be fixed. You consult another book or another friend or the doctor again. Do these problems ever go away? Are they all fixable? My thoughts are no. My thoughts are that parenting is a big ping pong game. Each day bringing different challenges than the day before and balls keep coming at you whether you are prepared with a paddle or not. Bing, bing … bing, bing, bing … each ball a new and different challenge. One day, you feel like you've got it figured out, only to be laughed at by the universe the next day. I'm not saying that books can't help us all be better parents (I've used more than I can count) but, it's so frustrating that there is no perfect book for the entire dilemma or family drama that exists in your world; no book that fixes it all!

I once e-mailed an out-of-town friend about a crazy morning I had. I was so proud of keeping my cool and handling the situation like any book would have suggested (I even used several strategies I had pulled out of my most recent read). I suppose I should have waited to send that e-mail until about 4:00 that afternoon. By then, I had done everything any book would suggest NOT to do. The afternoon catastrophe was a similar situation as the morning, but unfortunately a totally different outcome. Geez! Can you win in this thing called parenting? And who has time to find a book to solve each problem? No book is made to order just for you and your family dynamics or one that masters how to perfectly parent all the different personalities your children are blessed with.

The reason for there not being a manual out there that tells you how to raise the perfect child is because there is no perfect child. There is no perfect way to parent. The way I do it may not work for you and your family. And that's okay! Books are great resources, friends are amazing resources, doctors are board certified resources, but none of these resources can tell you what your parenting philosophy should be or give you a minute-by-minute playbook dictating how to handle the crises that come up (and they will). I suppose if you don't have daily struggles or crises that *you* should write a book on what you've done as the perfect parent (I'd probably read that one, too, hoping to fix all our limitations).

The best parenting advice I've heard, "This too shall pass!" Stages come and go, struggles come and go, but your parenting job never ends and you've got to find what works for you. What works for you may not be in the best-seller parenting book and that's okay.

Best Bribe

The book said I shouldn't bribe my child, but the author obviously hadn't been sleep deprived for the last ten years like I had.

From day one, my son would not sleep. Nights, naptime ... sleeping was a struggle, a battle and no fun for me or my husband. I read all the books and tried to do all the right things, but nothing would get that kid to sleep. If we did get him to sleep, he was in our room within hours. I reread all those books, talked with other mothers and wore out every strategy I could think of. Nothing would work. By the time he was ten, we were at our wits end. We were ready to send our son off to sleep training school like we sent our dog off to behavior class.

We went through night lights, holding the door shut, super nanny idea after super nanny idea. We even tried scooting closer and closer to the door each night away from his bed. I remember one night having him lay in his bed, me lying in my bed down the hall with my arm on the night stand so he could see my arm, hoping that would help his anxiety and allow him to fall asleep. Funny enough, that didn't work either. Finally, I decided a counselor was needed. We had this nice woman who came to the house and tried to give us some techniques to help. *That* didn't work either.

At age ten, my son wanted a cell phone more than he could stand. I was completely opposed to the idea and was not planning to give in to his desires. One night, feeling over-tired, overwhelmed and not wanting to fight another sleep battle, I begrudgingly threw out a bribe. If he went to bed and stayed in his bed for ten nights in a row, he could have the darn phone. I knew this wouldn't work, but secretly hoped I could get at least one night of peace.

We had been fighting this battle for ten years. I began to think the kid would never be able to sleep through the night or sleep away from home. Well, sure as you know what, that kid went to bed nice as pie every night for ten nights. He never woke me up for ten nights. Apparently, he slept through the night (for the first time in his entire life) for ten nights. Needless to say, my son got his phone. He's been sleeping just fine ever since. Forget the books. Bribery is the answer! It's Okay.

Child Lock

The book said I could lock my child in his room, but it didn't say how that would be perceived by others.

So picture a large group of elementary educators standing around prior to a staff meeting, commenting on the lack of parenting happening in the world today. Then picture the ever-so-sweet elementary guidance counselor (that's me), offering the parental viewpoint. Trying my hardest to help them all see the other side of the story and that parenting really is more difficult than it looks. Trying to convince them that the student they see at school might not be the son/daughter these parents see at home.

Earlier that day I had been visiting with one particular co-worker about her own toddler and struggles she was having. I seemed to be having similar struggles with my toddler (well, okay, four-year-old) and so we brainstormed what to do. I had shared that one book I read suggested that you could give your child a time-out in his room with the choice of having his door open or closed; that would make him feel like he had control. If he came out of his room (which he ALWAYS did), you could give him the choice of having his door locked or unlocked. Yes, we switched the door knobs so that we could lock the door from the outside! This co-worker confessed that she had locked her child in his room also and felt so much better that the 'counselor' had done this, too. She was confessing just as another educator walked by and heard about the *counselor locking her kid in his room*. Little did I know this confession would lead to some major embarrassment later that afternoon?

The joke was definitely on me later that day at our staff meeting. As I was preaching to my fellow educators before our staff meeting began to not judge and to consider the difficult job parenting is, the educator that heard the earlier confession shouted out (by now, almost the whole staff was around). "Maybe we should just suggest to our parents that they lock their kids in their rooms." Okay, totally taken out of context. All eyes were on me. Everyone looked, gasped and couldn't believe it. "YOU? NOT YOU!" They all seemed to say in disbelief that this sweet and gentle counselor might have to resort to locks. Well, it worked and in my defense, the book said it was okay.

Hey, I'm human. I yell. I scream. My kids can be crazy. They might behave in public (sometimes), but all hell breaks loose at home. Yes, yes, yes. I had to turn my son's lock around on his door. The kid was the busiest beaver I had ever laid eyes on. He wouldn't listen to a word I said. Curious George got into less trouble than my son. So, what did I do? I did what all good parents do and I read a book. Granted, while the book had great ideas, I definitely did not follow the plan consistently. The lock seemed to work for a short while, but then a new strategy had to be put in place. These educators would be happy to know that it was not corporal punishment, and my son now takes breaks without being dragged kicking and screaming. The lock hasn't been used in years (at least not for him, anyway!). It's Okay.

Not the Kindergarten Kind

The books didn't know my kid.

At the time I thought it was the most profound parenting decision I would ever make. Little did I know what was to come after my little lady grew into an adolescent? So I had to decide, should I send my youngest daughter to kindergarten as a soon-to-be five-year-old or should I hold her back? I read all the differing opinions from the experts, suffered great angst as I listened to my friends who had mapped out their children's educational careers through their PhD programs and was torn as to what to do. According to my friends, their children would be so bored in school if they were held back and worse, it would later be devastating to their self-esteem. Ugh, my friends were supposed to know it all (or at least their resources were supposed to be accurate).

I knew my daughter was right on the edge; socially mature, relatively well behaved, knew her ABCs and able to tie her shoes. What more could you ask from a kindergartner? Besides that, she had been in Montessori pre-school for two years. What other evidence did I need to convince myself to send her early? Yet, there was this nagging little guilt eating at me. Was I sending her early because she was academically ready or because I wanted time to myself?

I talked with my oldest child's veteran first grade teacher, who would be teaching kindergarten the next school year. She gave me excellent advice: send your daughter to kindergarten round-up and the staff will give you their opinion. Whew! Off the hook! I wouldn't have to decide. My daughter reluctantly went to kindergarten round-up and I secretly hoped the teachers would tell me that she was SO ready for kindergarten. I had already begun a list of projects I wanted to accomplish once school started.

The time had arrived. Kindergarten round-up was over and I went up to school to get my ready-to-be-a-kindergartener. When I walked in I noticed the staff smiling at me and several came over to meet me. Wow! Like any mother, I knew my children were incredible, but my daughter must have impressed the pants off them. The list of projects I was going to complete was growing longer and longer.

The teacher said my daughter did well, but she was quiet and not interacting with any of the other kids or staff. Then the teacher spilled the beans, prefacing it with telling me what a good laugh the staff got out of the only time my daughter talked that day. Hmmm! I mentally crossed off the wallpaper project that was at the top of my list. Apparently when the kids were busy coloring, one of the staff members walked over to my daughter and innocently asked, "What's your name?" My smarty-pants four-year-old looked up and said, "Read the name tag." As all the adults in the room enjoyed one last laugh, I mentally crumpled up the list of projects I was so eagerly waiting to start.

While that little episode was not the defining factor in my decision to hold her back, it convinced me that I wanted to enjoy my little girl a while longer before the rat race of school officially began. I felt at peace knowing that holding her back would not jeopardize her academic future or cause her to resent me later in life for being the oldest in her class. Turns out neither the books, nor my friends knew what was best for my little lady. Only I did!

Years later, I can look back at my decision fiasco and laugh. My daughter's never been the oldest in her class and she's pretty happy that she will be one of the first in her grade to drive a car. Why didn't I think of that? Although she is not an academic superstar, my daughter's teachers consistently tell me what a mature, responsible, hardworking student she is. What more could a mom ask for? Holding her back is the best parenting decision I have made to date; though, there are many others still in question! It's Okay.

Household Hazards

The books say you shouldn't worry about keeping up on the house and just spend time with your kids ... but then who is going to maintain this place we call a home?

The books talk about how important it is to spend time with your newborn, sleep when your baby is sleeping and later to spend time playing with your children. They tell you not to worry about the sink full of dishes or that closet that needs to be gone through. Seems easy, right? According to the books, having kids tremendously reduces your household responsibilities ... perfect. If only the world really worked like that. If only I had a Fairy Godmother to take care of every household task and detail that overwhelm me daily.

Seriously, did the authors of these books have people clean their homes? Did they have accountants who did their budgets and maintained their bills and finances? Did they have servants that picked up the endless amounts of crap that gets dropped in every corner? And this doesn't even touch the laundry or the lawn care or the vehicle maintenance. How on earth do people find time to sleep when their babies are napping or to just sit and play with their children while still completing the daily tasks that make life functional?

I wish I had just one story to share about this philosophy of 'letting things go' but unfortunately, I have a story for about every three weeks that pass. Each time I undertake the job of cleaning and organizing the house, I decide that I will just do a little each day so that I will have time to 'play' with the children. I 'let go' of the idea that the house will look neat and clean, I 'let go' of the laundry for a few days, I 'let go' of doing the dishes after each meal. And then, ALL HELL BREAKS LOOSE.

How do people do it? Life never ends. There are always a thousand and two things to do. And as soon as you do most of them, a thousand more things come up. There has to be a better way than to just 'let it go'! If I skip laundry for a few days or leave the dishes in the sink, it takes twice as long to complete the tasks when I actually get to them. Plus, I'm on edge and more agitated because I know it's going to take longer than if I would have actually just done them when they needed to be done.

The books are right about a few things. Parents do need to be rested and parents should find time to just 'enjoy' their children. But really, if the books are going to suggest this, there should be several other chapters that outline all the other stuff that makes up parenting and keeps the home front functioning! 'Letting it go' hasn't quite worked for me, but I sure am trying.

One morning I looked like a particularly harried mom racing around getting my children ready for their day. Lunches made? Check! Clean clothes on? Check! Teeth brushed? Check! Beds made? Check! Homework in backpacks? Check! Breakfast served? Check! Check, check, check! Plus I needed a cup of coffee. My loving son looked up at me as I was working on hair-do number three while my daughters were eating at the breakfast table. My squirt bottle, comb and hair ties were all in hand, "Mom, why don't you ever just sit down and eat breakfast with us?"

Adult temper tantrum? Check! I rattled off every minor detail that needed to be complete for our family world to function. My boy ignored my fit, "Yeah, but you have all day to do all that other stuff. You should really just sit down and eat with us while we are here."

Well, maybe the books aren't all wrong. I sat down that morning, ate with the kids and have made more of an effort since. There will always be a sink full of dishes needing to be washed, a load of laundry needing to be done, a budget needing to be balanced and a bed needing to be made. There will always be stuff to do, but my children will continue grow and I don't want to look back and think that I wasted any time with them. I'm a work in progress, and apparently so is my house. It's Okay.

Nursing Not's

*The books say that nursing is a beautiful, joyful thing …
but, I don't agree!*

Oh, the nursing books. Feeding your baby from the breast is best. Formula is evil, right? Well, nursing is not always the joyful picture that is painted for you on the hospital murals. It is not always that amazing bonding moment, when you look peacefully into your child's eyes and instantly connect. It's hard. It's work. It takes commitment. Nursing was a battle that I was willing to fight and it was a battle that I was *not* going to lose.

When my daughter was twelve weeks old, I headed back to work. I had done my best to get a supply saved up (like the books suggested) and I had my scheduled times that I was going to pump. Unfortunately, I could either pump in my car or the bathroom, neither of which was the most pleasant experience, but like I said, I was going to win this battle! I fought and fought. It was not easy, but I made it through the next six months until I had some time off from work again where I could reestablish this wonderful nursing bond. Ha!

At about seven months old, my daughter became a very fidgety nurser. She was never great at it, like the books said she would be, but once she became mobile, things were wild. She wouldn't just squirm around when she ate, she would stand up, sit on me, hit me, scratch me, pull my hair and crawl all over. Again—this is not like what the pictures in the books or murals highlight!

When she was about ten months old, my husband and I were to take a trip. I should have known that nursing on the plane was not a good idea, but I did it anyway. Luckily, my husband and I were the only adults in our row and I thought it would be a good time to feed her quickly. I threw on my nursing cover and headed into battle. My daughter was particularly displeased about a cover being over her head and started flailing her arms about. I only wish that I could have seen a video of the whole thing. Limbs were coming out of every opening and every minute or two, her head popped up through any part of the fabric she could nudge out of her way.

I am sure the flight attendant got more than she bargained for that day. Many men have paid for less of a show, but hey, she got fed. My husband and I could not stop laughing and thought the whole scene was quite humorous. One thing I couldn't learn from a book, but rather from experience, is that you have to be able to laugh at yourself. Parenting is too hard and you'll never make it unless you learn to giggle with the best of 'em! It's Okay.

Pulled Over

The book said I should take a time-out on the side of the road if my kids misbehave in the car, but it didn't say that a Good Samaritan would pull over and make me look like a complete idiot!

Okay, is there anything worse than trying to drive when you have fighting, whining, crabby kids in the back of the car? Threatening time-outs when we got home hadn't seemed to do the trick. Most of the time going home instead of our destination was not an option. Screaming seemed to only escalate the problem. Slamming on the breaks could only end in disaster. What do parents do? My kids were only four, three and one. What was going to happen when they were teens?

Having our third child rocked our parenting world in a way that no one could have imagined. It's safe to say that our house was in complete chaos for about a year and a half. We lost total control of our older two and while this new baby was ever so sweet, she started rolling her eyes at people by the ripe old age of nine months. She may have been a sweet baby, but that was long gone before the age of one.

We did what all desperate parents do. We read a book. Well, okay, I read a book and then told my husband what he was supposed to do. It was supposed to be like a 'book study' type thing that turned into me doing his homework. Anyway, I digress; we read a wonderful parenting book about giving kids three chances and then taking a break once their three consecutive or not consecutive chances had been blown. Great, I thought we could be consistent with this; easy as pie. There was even a section for the car—bonus!

So, picture our three grabby gooses, three wide across the backseat of the car. Obviously this was our first issue ... why would we have put them all next to each other? Anyway, I was solo and driving them to a family party when one kid started something. The whining, then the screaming ensued. I looked in the rearview and calmly told them, "That's one for all of you." I can do this, I thought to myself. Quickly, I tried to envision everything the chapter on the car had said, wanting to make this work more than anything. Then I saw an elbow, heard a shriek and realized one kid just got popped in the mouth. Still calm, I told them, "That's two for all of you." I tried to remind them, though they couldn't hear me over their shouting, that if they got to three, I would have to pull the car over for a time-out (like the book said) and we would be late for the party.

Kicks hit the back of my chair, I couldn't hear the radio over the screaming and all control was lost. I was on a highway. I wanted to lose it on them, throw a major adult temper tantrum. But, I didn't. The book said we could take a time-out just like at home. The time would start when they were calm. They could sit as long as they needed. "I can do this," my mantra playing over and over in my head. I checked to make sure the shoulder could hold us, put my blinker on and pulled off the road. It was a highway. What if we get hit? What if someone doesn't see us? Okay, hazards on. I reminded them calmly that their third chance was blown, that their time would start when they were all quiet and that we were going to be late for the party. Then I threw in a jab, "But, go ahead and take as long as you need."

It was actually kind of working. They were calming down. Time hadn't technically started yet, but hey, they couldn't tell time. And then it happened. The part the book DIDN'T talk about; The Good Samaritan. Seriously? Why me? He was so kind. He pulled over, walked up to the window and ever-so-sweetly asked how he could help. I was mortified. I had my hazards on. Something was obviously the matter. I tried to explain. He looked at me more horrified than if I had actually blown a tire or something. What do the books know anyway? As soon as he left, I let my kids have it; preaching about what caused this major embarrassment. They probably didn't understand a word I said, but the tone did the trick. Adult temper tantrums sure feel good sometimes, even though they aren't that productive! One thing is for sure, they rode in silence the rest of the way to the party. It's Okay.

Addicted

The book said I should take my child's pacifier away before he turned three, but it didn't say how to take it away from my three-year-old when my new baby still needed one.

It's definitely easier to take a pacifier away from a one-year-old than a three-year-old, this I know from experience. While it's the ideal to take the pacifier away early, it's not always a battle that parents want to fight. There's teething, ear infections, potty training, etc. The list is endless about why pacifiers stay in the homes of so many parents and the mouths of so many children. It's too easy to give in as parents and while the books might make it seem like it shouldn't be an issue at all to take a pacifier from a child, it definitely became an issue in our house.

With our first child, we did everything by the book. Off the bottle by a year, pacifier gone by about ten months, success with the big kid bed by 18 months, potty trained before two; we thought this parenting thing was a breeze. Well, child number two was a different story all together and number three threw us for a loop not even a trained circus animal could get around.

When child number three was born, our second child was almost two years old. He was off the bottle, but that was about the only successful thing we had accomplished. The potty training was a joke, the big kid bed was even funnier and the pacifier was still glued to his mouth! By the time our third child was nine months old and our second child was nearing his third birthday, we knew it was time for a change. While the toilet was only used for pee (he still had to poop in his diaper) and the bedtime routine was a complete disaster, we had hope that we might find a tiny achievement in taking away the pacifier. The pacifier fairy visited our house and took the last pacifier (well, HIS last pacifier anyway).

We actually believed that things were going well with the pacifier. That is until we found the stash under his pillow. He didn't care that the baby pacifiers were smaller; they were just what he needed. Okay, stash found, stash gone!

We had hopes that our second try at ridding him of his pacifiers would be better.

We thought it was so sweet that every morning our boy would go and greet his baby sister; we thought the intentions were genuine—NOT! Although the pacifier stash from under his pillow was gone, the boy knew how to get his fix. He would wake up early, sneak into the baby's room and suck away on one of her pacifiers. Suck, suck, suck! Then back in the crib it would go. He was like an addict getting his fix. It took us a while to catch on, but one morning I witnessed the entire thing. He also started sneaking behind furniture, into another room or just around the corner. Fix after fix all day long. He'd suck, suck, suck and then put it back before we would notice.

Our third and final try to rid our three-year-old of his pacifiers ended with discarding every pacifier in the house. Our poor baby had to find other ways to self-sooth. Come on books! Throw us parents a bone. Try to understand that it's not as easy as it looks or sounds. The aftermath of creating a major change in a kid's life is unimaginable. Our poor boy, the middle child, the only boy; all he wanted was a pacifier! We were left with a sad little guy and a crabby baby, but I guess we should have been proud that we won a battle (especially since there were so many other battles that still needed to be fought). It's Okay.

Carrier Catastrophe

The book said I shouldn't put the baby carrier or bouncy seat on the table; I guess I know why ... now!

So the books always say that you should never set a baby on a counter while he or she is in any type of car seat or bouncy seat. I got that, I understood it. My first child was never on a counter or a table or even a couch. We would go someplace and I would carefully place my baby carrier on the floor. It was easy with one kid to follow rules and do what is suggested.

Well, when I had child number two, it wasn't that easy. My three-year-old was excited to have a baby brother. He wanted to touch him and hold him and play trucks with him. The only problem was that his baby brother was only a week old at the time. I was adjusting to being a mother of two; trying to entertain my oldest and still tend to my new baby. Life still required that I cook and clean and complete daily household tasks. Things were not easy, but we were making it.

Because my oldest was always in his brother's space, I started putting the carrier up on the table. That way, my older boy could keep going with his tasks and hopefully forget about the baby. One afternoon, I was preparing to leave the house. This always felt like I was packing for a week at Disney—making sure the diaper bag had all the essentials for the new baby and making sure I was stashed with things to entertain a three-year-old, as well.

Just needing to grab one more thing, I looked around and saw that my three-year-old was standing on a kitchen chair looking at and singing to the sleeping baby. Great! I thought this would buy me the minute I needed to clear the last part of the counter and grab the extra item for the diaper bag. Moving like the speed of lightening, taking the extra 30 seconds that I needed, I felt almost proud of the work I had accomplished that morning. Being a parent of two wasn't so bad. I was beaming and cheered to myself, "I can do this!"

CRASH! BOOM! BANG! BAM! I don't know the word to describe the sound I heard. But, I knew exactly what it was. Horrified, I moved like no other mother had moved before. The baby carrier was upside down on the floor. Disturbing images of what had just happened started to flash through my mind. I tried to push them all away, but my heart had plummeted to the bottom of my stomach.

I was certain the baby had slammed his head on the floor, positive that my child was going to be brain damaged for life. I flipped the carrier back over, expecting the worst. I was shocked to find my baby still sound asleep in the car seat. Thank goodness the baby was so tiny, praise the good Lord that he had been buckled in correctly! Not one part of his body had touched the kitchen floor when his car seat plummeted off the table.

Needless to say, we learned new ways to keep our three-year-old away from the baby. There is a reason why you aren't supposed to put those contraptions on counters and tables. In this case, the books may have been right; it'd only have been helpful if there were also suggestions as to what to do with the other kid in my house. It's Okay.

Nursing Nuisance

The books say you should nurse your child, but they don't exactly suggest what to do with your other children while a newborn is strapped to your boob!

Summer time is sweet for many reasons: swimming, picnics and park time. But, best of all, summer time is sweet because of a visit from our dear friends. This particular summer we had created a marvelous plan for a nine day adventure. Our friends loaded up their mini-van and headed on the eight hour trek to our house. We worked it out so that my friend and her children would stay the whole nine days while her husband flew home for the work week. My husband planned to work during the week as well, so we had both weekends with the husbands around and five days in the middle where just the mamas and the kiddos could play!

The week was going quite well and we had found plenty of time to gab. The only thing that ever seemed to get in the way were those darn children. There were seven of them for us to tend to that year. I might also mention that two of them were under six months of age and still nursing. Our three older children were doing a tremendous job and our two three-year-olds were doing okay. Well, I'll be honest; they were a lot of work. But, the two babies couldn't have been sweeter, and made up for the ornery three-year-olds.

On day five of our nine-day adventure, we were sitting on the couch nursing our babies, and gabbing about one thing or another. The three older children had started a make believe game in the basement and the two three-year-olds were at the table coloring. I might add that the three-year-olds were doing an outstanding job. The house was actually quiet and there was some peace in the air.

No one did anything wrong, there was no action that we could have scolded for, but a definite problem ensued. One of the three-year-olds was coloring while sitting on a bench; a regular old bench that fits at a kitchen table. He happened to be on his knees with his toes curled around the back side of the bench. He leaned over to get a crayon and the bench slipped. We heard the bench, we heard the screeching, but really assumed that there was minimal damage and that the boy was just over-reacting.

Being a kind and decent friend (since this was technically my bench), I stopped nursing, put my baby down and went to assess the damage. Ever so calmly I walked into the kitchen. I was greeted by a screaming child. The three-year-old that wasn't mine was running around the table and towards me. Blood was flailing with every step he took. My calmness came to an end as I shouted, "Oh, my God. **Oh, my God!**" Talk about the worst reaction ever. Thank goodness for his mother.

She was like Super Mom. She dislodged her baby from her boob, scooped up her three-year-old and put him over the sink to calm him down. Blood was EVERYWHERE! My husband happened to come home from work early that afternoon, thank the good Lord, so we appointed him to be the driver. The other six kids didn't know what to think of the craziness and were so scared for their friend and brother. Super Mom and Dad-who-wished-he-would-have-stayed-at-work headed for the hospital.

After 13 stiches, lots of bandages and several months of healing, the boy's toe was almost completely back to normal. Our friends opted not to sue and our bench became off limits for the next year. While I will forever have guilt about that bench and the boy's poor toe, it all goes back to the books. Here we were, doing the right thing; nursing our babies and engaging our older children in activities that were pleasant and educational. We *still* almost lost a toe. Where's there a book for that one? It's Okay.

Partners Parts

The books say it's natural for kids to explore ... but COME ON!

In the previous story you read about our dear friends who we see about once a year. You might think they would have smartened up and opted NOT to come back to our house after nearly losing a toe, but alas, the following summer, they came back to visit yet again. This time, though, the husbands decided to stay far, far away from the trouble that might ensue. They packed up and headed north to fish in the Boundary Waters where they couldn't even be reached by cell phone.

I wish I could say that this story was about someone other than the three-year-old who was a bloodied mess the previous summer, but I can't. At least this story doesn't include any blood or missing parts. It does, however, include body parts; body parts that should stay beneath the undergarments parents provide. It's funny how parenting and child development books state that it's 'normal' for children to be curious about the private parts of the body. As parents, though, we are left with a vague understanding as to how much exploration is actually 'normal'.

You might remember a mention about the three-year-olds being a lot of work. Well, they were now four; but just as naughty as they were the previous summer. Seven kids were again in our four-bedroom house. Our family included three girls and a boy and their family included three boys. Surely, there was bound to be some exploration, especially since all these children were under the age of seven. Well, wanting to catch up, my friend and I let them play without supervising their every move. Some might say it was poor parenting; we would play the card that at least they were just 'sniffing'!

The two four-year-olds (one boy and one girl) were hot and cold all week. Either loving each other or hating one another; either trading her sparkly skirt for his boy shorts or fighting over the same toy. They went upstairs to have a 'meeting'. They wanted time to 'talk'. Maybe this should have thrown up red flags, but again, we were too busy chatting. The two of them were actually getting along. Who would worry?

Apparently, we should have been more worried than we actually were! It had been quiet. Too quiet! I finished up one of my many stories shared that week and went up to see what was happening. As I opened the door, there was squirming and looks of horror. Oh my, there were no pants on. Keeping my cool, I asked, "What are you two doing and why are you not wearing any pants?" In unison, the two whispered, "Nothing." I provided a short rant about appropriateness and trust and who knows what else.

Finally, my little girl came clean. "We were just sniffing each other's butts! It was HIS idea!" I turned, desperate to gain my composure, trying to hold back the laughter and the tears. "You two get your pants on right now. We are going to have to do something about this; I just don't know what yet." I looked sternly at the young boy. "You need to go down and tell your mother what happened. She's going to be very disappointed." I jetted out of the room as quickly as possible. I nearly tripped down the stairs I was moving so fast. I had to warn my dear friend about what our children were up to and get my giggles far out of the way before her boy came down to confess. It's Okay.

CHAPTER IV

My Life Is Nothing But Poop, Pee And Puke

There is absolutely nothing in life that can prepare you for all the revolting, gut wrenching, nauseating, disgusting, horrendous fluids that parents have to deal with. Snot, vomit, blood, feces, spit, drool! Seriously the list never ends. Not only do you have to deal with it as a parent, you have to find it days, weeks or months later stuck to cars, chairs and even between leg fat.

To be honest, it's probably good you don't really know what you are getting into before you become a parent. Chances are you would think that you couldn't handle it and give up on this parenting hoopla before it even started. You can handle it; you do handle it, but goodness, it's best if those outside your family don't know what truly happens behind closed doors. And it's best if those outside of the bathroom stall don't really know what is happening in that public restroom.

Embarrassment, shame, humiliation; these are the feelings that are most evident when dealing with pee, poop and puke. It's not so bad if other people don't really know what's happening, but when they do, there is not a more mortifying moment. I mean everyone poops, but somehow when your child pukes or has a blow-out or sneezes so hard snot drips down to his toes, it happens to be the most inopportune moment; when you're around your germ-freak friend, the co-worker that doesn't have kids or the store clerk that has to clean up the mess you've just created. Not only is your kid disgusting, but now that person somehow has less respect for you! Not much you can do about the three P's ... except laugh and then disinfect! It's Okay.

Smelly Butts

So, we all poop. It's life. Before I had kids, I was somewhat disgusted by how moms would check to see if their kids needed a diaper change. I'd be with my friends who had kids and one of the moms would smell poop. Immediately, one of them would say, "Is that my stinky kid?" Then as if synchronized, they would all scoop up their children and either shove their noses in their kids' butts or stick their fingers down the back side of their diapers to see whose kid had done their business. To a person without children, this is a little revolting.

Two kids later, I now laugh at my ever-conservative husband. I'll ask him to check and see if one of the kids has a dirty diaper. He will, without fail, scoop up the child, walk up the steps to the changing table, pull down the pants, unfasten the onesie, undo the diaper strip by strip and check. The process takes no less than two minutes and sometimes more.

I, on the other hand, have turned into that mom who simply picks up the kid, shoves her nose against the butt, smells and determines the course of action. My method takes only two seconds and hasn't failed me yet! I've proudly become one of those parents I used to be disgusted by. It's Okay.

Not Faultless

I took the day off from work to accompany my son on a 5th grade field trip to some sort of outdoor experience. It was unseasonably cold. In fact the power had gone out that morning. We actually got interviewed by one of the local TV stations as we entered the school asking us what it was like getting ready without power. It was a pretty cool way to start the field trip! If only the day would have ended that wonderfully.

As we were getting dressed, I was very concerned that my son was going to be too cold. "We're going to be outside all day long, you need to be dressed for the weather." I have to admit, I may have gone a little overboard, and hindsight is always 20/20. I made him put on some of *my* tights under his jeans, two pairs of socks, three layers of shirts and his big puffy jacket.

As we headed off to the field trip, I began to realize that my son may have been a tad overdressed. By the time we made it to the first stop on our field trip and got out to walk around, he was already hot. "Mom, why did you make me wear all of this stuff?" No biggie, I thought. I told him to go into the bathroom and take off the tights. Problem solved, right? Wrong. Just then the teacher announced that we were running behind schedule, so we would be eating our sack lunches on the bus, while driving to our next destination. Oh, no. Not a good thing. Not good at all. My overdressed, hot son, who was unable to take off the tights, used to get terribly carsick. Lunch in the moving bus ... while being hot? I could smell disaster brewing.

We ate our lunch and then it began. "Mom, I'm not feeling good, I'm going to be sick." Not a second later, he started throwing up. Not just a little gagging, but huge, spewing, projectile vomit. I didn't want him to embarrass himself, so I tried to 'hide' the fact that he was throwing up. Obviously I made many errors in judgment that day. I took off my coat and tried to catch his vomit. Of course, that didn't work and it started spilling over the sides of my coat and onto the floor. The puke was running under the seats. The girls in the seat ahead of us started to notice the puke as it was running under their shoes. They started to freak out. I, of course, chimed in, thinking I could still salvage the smidgen of reputation my son had left. "It's just throw-up. It's okay." By that point, the whole bus lost control. They all knew. "Yuck, he's throwing up!" The teacher got a plastic garbage bag, but unfortunately he was done puking by then.

To this day, my son still teasingly blames me for overdressing him that day, causing the vomit incident. As soon as I saw the other kids at school, I knew he was overdressed. Combine that with his tendency to be car-sick and it was double-trouble. I learned a lesson that day; that I used to over-think things too much. My kids were always the most prepared, had the most stuff in case anything went wrong, the heaviest backpack, etc. The puke taught me a lot! I needed to let them live and learn—on their own. It's Okay.

Highchair Horror

Poo-splosion, poo-mageddon, poo-pocalypse, poo-nami. No matter what you call it, you can count on one thing as a parent; you are going to deal with a lot of poo. This will range from projectile poo on the wall at 2:00am to diaper explosions that are up the back and seeping out the front. I cannot track the great deal of poo I had already experienced in my daughter's ten months of existence. There is, however, one particularly memorable poo-catastrophe that I will never forget.

It all started in the glorious, just cleaned highchair. My daughter was already down to a diaper and bib; it was one of those messy days. She was eating, well okay, she was making a disaster with her food and I decided to help. I reached down to pick up a piece of food that had fallen in her seat and my hand encountered something warm and wet. This wasn't good. Not good at all. She was supposed to be eating solids. I quickly pulled my hand out to find it coated in the most disgusting looking poo I had seen yet.

The poo was squishing out both the top and side of her diaper. Instead of calmly cleaning up the unmistakable explosion, I panicked. I screamed. Oh, thankfully my husband was there to rescue me. Together, we frantically went over our options for the highchair extraction. Ultimately we decided to bite the bullet and pick her up to fully assess the damage. That was mistake number one. As soon as I picked her up, poo started dripping on the floor. That led to mistake number two. We hadn't put the dog away. Horrified, I yelled at my husband to keep the dog away and ran with my poo-dripping daughter to the trashcan. Mistake number three … why did we buy a trashcan with a lid?

My husband proceeded to take off the diaper over the trashcan and wipe off what he could. To finish the clean-up, we rinsed her little buns in the kitchen sink using the water sprayer. Needless to say, I never thought my kitchen sink would encounter such germs! Although this method may have been a tad unorthodox, in our defense, she ended up clean. It's Okay.

Duct Tape or Die

It all started when our quadruplets turned one. Yes I said quadruplets! You can close your mouth now. We are doing great. Anyway, they had always shared a room from the first day they came home from the hospital. They learned to sleep quite well together from an early age. Most mornings, one of them would wake up, stand up in the crib, make some noises, jump up and down and wake up another brother. This would start the ripple effect of goofing off, laughing out loud and entertaining one another until all four were a part of the fun. This fun would let us know they were ready for their day to begin and would signal the end to our morning peace.

One morning was different. We heard them wake up, goof off, and then nothing. It was quiet, too quiet. We were still too new to the parenting game to know that whenever it is quiet, something really bad must be happening. This quiet morning changed our mornings for many, many months.

When we opened the bedroom door ten minutes later, there was an unusual look on all of the boys' faces. They all stood up, not jumping loudly to be taken out of their cribs, but very slowly like robbers being caught in the alley behind the bank. As they stood, one baby was naked, completely naked. His mattress was soaked, the carpet underneath his crib was wet and there we saw his diaper. The diaper was lying wide open on the floor next to his crib. As we approached his crib, the unusual, yet concerned look on his face, quickly changed to the proudest smile we had ever seen. We laughed hysterically, again not knowing the repercussions of this incident, put on a fresh diaper, cleaned the mattress, sheets and carpet and continued the day as normal. Little did we know, this was just the beginning of the 'Monkey See, Monkey Do' problem that was about to plague us.

The next day, two boys were naked. The next week, everyone was naked. So, idea number one began with snap onesies. One week later, one boy was naked. The next day, three boys were naked. Idea number two came to pass with shorts over the onesies. Three days later, two boys were naked. Idea number three had us buying four sleepers with zippers and snaps. One month later, one boy was naked. A week later, two boys were naked. Idea number four was a t-shirt over the sleeper with a zipper and a snap. Three weeks later, one boy was naked. The next week, three boys were naked. The next couple months were not funny and the nakedness was no longer cute.

So, as the boys approached their second birthdays, the nakedness continued to be a struggle. Clean up after clean up. Mind you, some of these were more than just pee, yuck. We tried to stay on top of the de-briefing as soon as they woke up from nap or night-time. They were transitioned to big boy beds. We were hoping to keep them from climbing out and falling on their heads. Then we had our next grand idea.

Idea number five was painters tape over the diaper tabs. Bright blue tabs should do the trick (or so we hoped). The new tabs were going to solve our problem. Two weeks later, one boy was naked. One day later, three boys were naked. Idea number six was to take the tape all the way around the waist; essentially a blue belt. Four days later, one boy was naked. Two days later, two boys were naked. They actually helped one another tear the tape from each other's diapers. The last idea we had before losing our minds was DUCT TAPE. We never used it in public, at least not when others could see. Two months later, it was hit or miss success with the new grey belts.

We have learned not to leave any spot un-taped to ensure they can't get into each other's pants! Poop, pee and puke fly in our house more than most and our struggles are often multiplied by four. But, we continue to adapt, and the strongest bond we have isn't duct tape. It's each other! It's Okay.

Bonfire Blunder

Well, since you got the background on our quadruplets in the previous story, from my husband's perspective, I felt there was one more great story that couldn't go untold. If you haven't figured it out yet, our four boys enjoyed taking off their diapers more than anything. This became a battle against Mom and Dad. These four ornery boys continued to take off their diapers and streak around their room, the house, really anywhere they could get away with it. The 'gray belts' worked wonders. That is, when they were actually around our children's diapers.

You know how parents talk about all those late night runs to get diapers and formula? Well, sadly, we had an experience where we needed to or should have run out for duct tape. When my husband and I left our boys with my mother (she is our amazing care-taker for the boys) one particularly calm morning, we all had our fingers crossed that this day would *not* be a diaper-off day. We hoped that maybe the boys would forget their 'Monkey See Monkey Do' trip and leave their parts in their pants.

After changing a particularly dirty diaper that afternoon, my mother quickly ran to dispose of the gut-wrenching smelly diaper in the garage. She could not have been gone more than 30 seconds. When she reentered the living room, she heard lots and lots of giggling. She looked and found that one of our boys had removed his diaper. He was standing next to the fireplace, peeing onto the logs. The other three sons stood by their brother, proud, each taking turns lifting their feet into the stream. Oh, the joys of having four boys the same age! It's Okay.

Graduation Gone Wrong

It was my oldest son's special day; kindergarten graduation. With all the hype they make about graduation from kindergarten, you'd think he was heading to Yale the following year. Anyway, my husband couldn't get off work and my in-laws who were supposed to attend had to cancel at the last minute. Feeling like my son wouldn't have any supporters, I unfortunately decided to take his two younger siblings. I was thinking this would increase his fan club. He was devastated that I would be the only one there. I couldn't wait until he saw who got added to the invite list.

The graduation started in the gym. It was there, within the first two minutes, that I realized bringing a two-year-old and a four-year-old to a kindergarten graduation ceremony was a big mistake. I was an emotional mess thinking that my oldest was already grown and headed out the door to college and then there were the two siblings, who were not at all interested in the activity at hand (nor did they care for my emotions). Leaving the gym, I already had sweat dripping down my back. The wrangling did not go well. The gym was just the beginning. We headed to the library, broke into smaller groups and were to listen to the kindergartners share stories they had written.

I quickly realized that I had a new role. I was supposed to get up with my kindergartner in front of the ten other students (and their fan clubs) to help him share his story. My two-year-old was in her stroller and my four-year-old was actually having a moment of silence. As I went to the front, my two-year-old immediately started to freak out and make an un-library-like scene. A saintly woman who had been seated next to us got her out of her stroller and sat her on her lap while we shared the story. Whew, made it! Did it! Fan club was a success after all.

Or maybe it was not! As I walked toward the saintly woman to retrieve my child, my little lady shouted, "Mommy, my pooped, my pooped!" Oh, it was not poop, it was what you might call an explosion.

I don't think I could have been redder and the sweat was no longer just rolling down my back. The next kindergartner had begun his book, so I ever so elegantly scooped up my two-year-old, dragged my four-year-old and tripped through the library lugging the stroller behind me. Poop was everywhere—up the back, down the leg, smeared on the belly—oh no. I had no clothes, but thank goodness for the back-up pull-up stuffed into the bottom of my purse. The graduation was only supposed to last an hour—my thoughts before were, "What can really go wrong in just an hour?"

Needless to say, we didn't make it back to the library for a while. My poor boy had to suffer through part of his graduation alone. My semi-clean, pull-up only two-year-old, got wheeled out through the main lobby for many bystanders to see. I had a spare t-shirt in the car. It was just enough to go back in and say good-bye. Thank goodness I didn't have to sit near the saint when I came back in and there is a God, because I haven't to this day run into her again. I am praying that her saintly behavior was enough to keep the explosion from reaching anywhere on her. I guess we will never know! It's Okay.

Pee, Poop AND Puke

It was my first day back to school as a kindergarten teacher. The children were bright-eyed and ready to learn. I was excited as could be to get the year started with such an amazing group of little people. I love my job and this first day of school could not have gone more smoothly. I started picturing what my year was going to be like with this new group and joy began to grow in my heart. As I walked the students out to meet their parents on the first day, I was beaming. My pride for my class showed as each student marched to his/her parent and began recounting the wonderful day.

My husband and I often had to swap our children at my school because he worked and took classes. The swap that happened this particular afternoon did not add to my great day, but rather destroyed my visions for a wonderful year. I was suddenly caught up in my own disaster and couldn't bear to give my school children one more thought.

Our youngest daughter had been home that day with a minor fever; nothing serious, we thought, and my husband and I were grateful he could take the day with her. There were few words shared as he dropped my older son and sick daughter in my classroom, and jetted off for work. Not two minutes into my children's drop off, my son wet his pants. Gee whiz, you've got to be kidding. I didn't even have a change of clothes. Thank goodness we were at a school with a nurse's office full of used clothes. Some over-sized pants would have to do the trick. Just as we were walking back to my classroom from the nurse's office, a horrendous smell passed by my nose. Ugh! My great day was going downhill quickly!

My sick, slightly fevered two-year-old had pooped in her diaper. Normally, this foul smell could have been cleaned up quickly and easily, but my adoring husband brought only wipes. Yes, that's right; I could wipe her down, but had no diaper to put on her freshly cleaned bottom! Again, thankfully, I was in a school. I sulked over to the preschool teacher's room, begging for a diaper or a pull-up. Maybe my luck was turning around, she had one to spare.

It was definitely time to go, before any other catastrophe could further spoil my day. I bagged up my son's sopping pants and my daughter's poop-stained outfit and practically jetted out the door. My kids were tripping over themselves trying not to get left behind in the school. We made it. We were buckled in and ready to go. Ten minutes into our 25 minute car ride home, any chance for my afternoon to turn around was shot. My son threw up all over the car. Not just a little vomit, but projectile vomit that shot onto the back of my seat (there may have even been a little in my hair, but I was too overwhelmed to notice). Seriously, you've got to be kidding me!

That night, our daughter was diagnosed with croup—so much for the minor fever. My son was home the next two days with the flu. And, I don't recall what happened to that bag full of dirty clothes. While there was nothing to do but laugh and cry, I couldn't help but take myself back to those hours before my own children arrived at my classroom door. I had had an awesome day before 3:00pm and some pretty cool kindergarteners I was blessed to teach. I suppose there is always a silver lining. It's Okay.

Dribbled

My husband was home alone with our boy just before he turned two. We were potty training our little man and were bound and determined to get that kid whipped into shape shortly after our second child was born. We didn't want to deal with two kids in diapers and he was ready. Well, he was ready to pee in the toilet. The poop became a very different story.

While my son caught on quickly to urinating in the toilet, he did everything he could to avoid going number two in that gigantic hole we called a potty seat. We soon gathered that when our son went missing for a short time, he was doing his business, somewhere other than on the toilet. We had heard that putting the 'big boy' underwear on might encourage him *not* to want to go in his pants. Really, it just created more of a mess for us to clean up because the poop still didn't get where it was supposed to go!

So, my husband was home alone with our boy. They were playing a game where my son would run from the front of the house back to his room and then come charging out for my husband to 'get' him. One venture back to his room took longer than it should have. My hubby quickly realized that he would probably find his 'big boy' pooping in the corner of his room and that he should be hasty in getting to his son. Screams of my son's name brought him running to the front room. With each step quickening, poop dribbled down his leg and onto the hallway floor. Step after step, dibbled poop after dribbled poop. Needless to say, the 'big boy' underwear did not hold much.

My husband scooped up his boy and darted for the bathroom, losing a couple turds along the way. As they were both getting washed up, my husband looked deep into our son's eyes. Surely there had to be some anger and frustration in those eyes. No words were spoken, except those that came from our son. "Dammit!" It was said under his breath. He had to know that is what his dad intended to say, so he just took care of saying it for him. It's Okay.

Pool Problem

Swim diapers are wonderful. That is, when your kid doesn't actually poop in them. Seriously, there is nothing worse than changing a swim diaper full of poop. At that point, I don't even know what you call it. It's all stuck to their stomach and back and bottom; the crap is everywhere. But, I have to admit, it is a joy to be able to take children swimming before they are potty trained, so I probably shouldn't complain. I'll keep my complaints to a minimum while I share this minor pool problem that turned into a major fiasco.

We were on vacation with our children and my husband's side of the family. There was a lake, some cabins and sights to see! It was wonderful. After five days part of the family departed and we were left with just our immediate family and the two grandparents. The day of the disaster, the grandparents were off doing their own thing, thank goodness, and it was just us. We decided it was a little cloudy and cold to hit the lake, so we instead ventured to the indoor pool.

I left my husband swimming with the kids while I took some alone time at the cabin to read. After almost a week of vacation, this was well deserved. But, after about ten minutes, I was feeling guilty and decided I should suck it up, put on my suit and enjoy vacation with my family. I wasn't quite up to jumping in the pool yet, but giggled and laughed with them while they were all swimming. A few minutes after I arrived, I noticed some brown stuff floating in the pool near the edge. I got closer and decided it was definitely poop. Immediately I jumped down my husband's throat. "Didn't you put a diaper on her?" He looked confused and was a little miffed that after leaving him to deal with the kids while I took a moment, I was now back only to rip on the work he had done. Of course he had remembered to put a diaper on the little lady, it was just apparently *not* working.

I grabbed the girl and tried to assess the damage. The bathroom was a good hundred feet from where I stood with her and the shower was just as far. I tried to move, but was frozen in shock about how to handle this catastrophe. I didn't want to put her too close to me and so with arms out straight, I ran as fast as I could to the bathroom. I might add that poop was dripping out with every step I took. I made it to the bathroom, only to discover that there was no trashcan. I backtracked about twenty feet and found a trashcan.

We had a minimal amount of wipes and to be honest, they wouldn't have done much good anyway. As gracefully as I could, which is not saying much, I disrobed my child of her suit and then tried to get her out of the faulty, poopy diaper. Once the diaper was in the trash, I headed for the shower. I rinsed her as best I could. It might be important to also mention now that the shower was *outside* of the bathroom, right in the middle of the pool walk way. I then glanced around and thanked the good Lord that we were still the only people in the pool area.

The other children were trying to be helpful, but I didn't want them to walk anywhere outside of the pool. I mean poop had leaked EVERYWHERE. But, I had to get them out of the pool, because it, too, was filled with poop. Ugh! "Just go stand over there," I think is what I instructed in the most unfriendly voice. After rinsing off the bare buns, I stuck her in the other side of the pool, hoping the chlorine would kill the remaining germs until we could properly shower her. I threw a diaper on her and tried to get her out of the way so we could assess the rest of the damage.

Not wanting to cause a major scene at the resort, my husband and I scanned the pool area for something to clean up the poop in the pool. The best thing I could come up with was the garbage lid. So, there in the pool, my husband scooped up piece of poop after piece of poop. He'd hand me the lid and I'd dump it in the garbage. This was all happening while still trying to keep the other kids out of the way and figure out what to do with the drippings that occurred while trying to dispose of the diaper.

What seemed like an eternity later, our family trudged back to the cabin, not talking at all about our shameful experience. Immediately, all the children were thrown in the shower to be properly washed. My husband was in the shower for a good twenty minutes, washing and rewashing, hopeful to wash away the memories of his pooper-picker-upper moments. It was awful ... absolutely awful. We never did figure out what happened with that faulty swim diaper, but one thing is for sure, the poop was everywhere but trapped inside. It's Okay.

Pee Puddle

Imagine me, a poor mother of four, who just got back from a week-end getaway with my husband. My husband was on a later flight due to his conference, so I was left alone with the kiddos for a few hours. I might add that this was the first getaway we had taken since having children. It had been almost eight years and was well deserved. I have to admit that I was still on a little high from being away and dreaded taking all four of my children to the store. I suppose a mother in her right mind wouldn't have left the house empty of food the day she left, but I had other things on my mind. Packing for four children to be away from their parents for two and a half days was like packing for a darn move!

I got all the kids picked up from their various locations and headed to the store. I made a pit stop along the way for burgers, secretly hoping this would increase their excitement for a trip to Wal-Mart after a long day at school. On the way to the store, my one-year-old started throwing a fit in the backseat. As it turned out, all she really wanted was the pop. So, pop it was. Here, have it—those were my thoughts. There rode my one-year-old with a large Diet Coke propped up in her lap, sipping away and delighted as could be. I know this is not the image of a mother who tends to her child's diet; maybe that's why she's off the growth charts!

Anyway, we got to the store and the one-year-old's lap was all wet. I assumed the wetness was due to the condensation on the pop. Later I found this to be an improper assumption (you know what they say about assuming?). So we made it through the store, without too many threats for time-outs at home. Two kids had lost a portion of their allowance, but who's counting? We were checking out—we were almost there. All parents know what a nightmare checkout is. You always hold your breath wondering what will go wrong. I had two playing with toys in the aisle, one buckled into the cart and one 'helping' me unload groceries. I was stepping rapidly over them, trying to get the groceries on the conveyer belt as quickly as I could. Of course, because I'm a cheap ass, I was also trying to sort the groceries for the ones I needed to price match. I dropped the list, found the list, sorted some more, stepped over a kid, pushed a kid out of the way, dropped the list again, sorted again, grabbed some more. Sweat was pouring down and I can't imagine what I looked like to those around me. Then, to top it all off, the one-year-old grabbed a box of candy and dumped it all over the floor.

One of the kids kindly helped me by picking up the candy. It was then that I noticed the pool of liquid below the cart. Crap, what was leaking? I asked the clerk to check the milks. They were fine. I looked at the juice. Nothing! Um! Oh well, no time to spare. I asked for paper towels, thinking this would keep two kids busy for a few minutes. It was then that I noticed some of the products in the cart were wet as well. Again, no time to worry, I could just wipe them down at home.

The clerk started to get concerned. "Did she have a sippy cup or anything?" I looked at my one-year-old strapped into the cart and my eyes got hooked on her soggy pants. It was then that something clicked; the wet pants earlier may not have been from the pop condensation. I kept my thoughts to myself as I continued to try to get the best deal, hand over my coupons and pay my bill. I just wanted to get out of the store. I knew why that liquid was on the floor and all over my groceries, but I sure as hell wasn't going to admit it. I was already mortified enough. Here I was shopping with four grabby gooses and looking completely overwhelmed. I couldn't stop to chat about what was really happening—that my daughter had just peed all over my groceries and the store floor.

It was then that I heard my four-year-old yell that she had to pee. Perfect, blessings do still exist. I instructed my seven-year-old to take her to the bathroom while I finished loading the groceries. "Make sure you wash your hands, **really well**," I shouted after them. Then I turned to my son. "Why don't you run to the bathroom, too? **Make sure to wash your hands**!"

I got out as quickly as I could, only briefly looking back to make sure the puddle had been cleaned sufficiently. So ... my kid's diaper had leaked. Well, not really leaked, rather not worked at all. She had completely peed through her diaper. Her pee was all over the store floor and, apparently, all over many of my groceries. We got home, unloaded the groceries and I began the wipe down. Needless to say, the one-year-old rode home in only a diaper and it's safe to say that the older kids figured out they had cleaned up their sister's urine and not some mystery liquid. We had food. I had a great weekend with my husband. Overall, it was a victory! It's Okay.

CHAPTER V

Delirious Decisions Due To Deprivation

Every parent has been there. If they say they haven't, they're flat out lying. I'm talking about the desperation for just one good night's sleep; heck, sometimes even five uninterrupted hours of sleep. Deprived of the very thing that helps our whole body function—sleep. There are times in the parenting world that a person feels as though they will NEVER know what it is like to be normal again; to be able to function without four cups of coffee in the morning and a caffeinated beverage at lunch.

This fog that parents live in at times cannot be healthy or safe! The working, cleaning and caring for your children; it's these monotonous parts of life that create no time for even a 15 minute cat nap. It's at these moments in life (and they eventually do pass) that desperation gets the better of us and we do things that are, at times, unimaginable. That's why we don't talk about them. How could you admit to the things you do when you are delirious? These things that you do, you do because you are unable to do anything else. It's simply survival.

Whether it's the middle of the night or the middle of the afternoon, sleep-deprived parents all over the world are doing some very unorthodox things to survive. Parenting becomes like survival of the fittest, unrested being. Which of these parents can hack no sleep, no break, no shower, no sex and no energy for healthy cooking? It's unrealistic. Parents do what they need to do to survive. *This too shall pass.* Wow, if only it would pass faster. It seems like you manage to get one aspect of a parent's deprived life figured out, only to be deprived in ten other ways.

What crazy things have you done in life when you weren't getting your doctor-recommended eight hours of rest every night? Will you admit it? Did you skip your shower to sleep ten extra minutes? Did you order an extra shot of espresso in your coffee? Did you fall asleep in a meeting or close your office door to get just five minutes of rest? Did you wear two different shoes or forget to put on your belt? From minor to major, every human has had to suffer through a day or two without good rest. Now add taking care of someone besides yourself to the mix.

Delirious decisions happen when you are unable to think clearly. These decisions come from being deprived of the sleep and time you need. Hey, it's okay.

Pacifier Strap

Being a first time parent had its challenges. Though, looking back, I can see that these challenges were nothing compared to what lay ahead in our parenting journey. I now have four children, six and under and one with special needs. Whew, if only I could go back to that moment when all I was worried about was the fact that my baby wouldn't take his pacifier.

I was a new mom of one and just wanting the fussiness to stop. If he wasn't sucking on something, well okay, sucking on me, then he was fussing. I just needed him to keep that darn pacifier in his mouth for more than ten seconds without it popping out. Then, maybe, I could get something done and give my poor boobs a rest. Or for goodness sakes, put in a load of laundry.

After trying every pacifier imaginable, I still couldn't get my son to keep the only thing that would be my savior in his mouth. One day, I had experienced one too many whimpers out of my little guy. I did the unimaginable. I threaded a piece of elastic through each hole on the pacifier. I made sure it wasn't too tight, but just right for that piece of plastic (his binky) to not escape from his suckle. The elastic went around his head and I am forever grateful to whoever invented the material.

While it may not have been the choice of most first-time moms, that piece of elastic saved me. It gave me the precious minutes I needed to accomplish the daily tasks necessary to live. It gave me those few extra hours of sleep I needed to function. It worked. And hey, later in life, I found that those elastic straps are used by medical professionals (though not to hold pacifiers in mouths) to hold masks in place during breathing treatments for kids. I wouldn't recommend this unconventional pacifier method, but I was delirious. It's safe to say that this was not the only crazy thing I have done as my four children are growing up happy and healthy. It's Okay.

Sleepy Shopping

For the first six weeks after giving birth to my third child, I did not attempt to venture out of the house much by myself. Just the thought of getting all three children in the car, strapped in and then out of the car and into any establishment, was entirely too overwhelming. I resorted to ordering groceries on-line and had them delivered to my door. I turned down play dates left and right and didn't even make park visits very often.

One day I had to get out of the house. What exactly was I afraid of? I went everywhere by myself with my first two kids. How different could this be? I could do one trip to the grocery store with my four-year-old, two-year-old and six-week-old. I started feeling like Super Mom, just imagining myself having a successful store visit. As I buckled them all in and started off on my journey, it was as if there was a cape on my back.

I was amazed at how well things were going at the store. Was anyone watching this? Were people secretly praising my mothering skills? I was elegantly pushing one cart with my three children in front of me and pulling a cart with groceries behind me. Thoughts of how great I was had me beaming. I couldn't believe I had spent the last six weeks cooped up inside my home, completely avoiding the world around me.

After forty five minutes of shopping was completed, all I needed to do was check out. The clerk rang up all my groceries and announced the total to me. I reached down to grab my wallet from the diaper bag when I realized it wasn't there. How could this be happening? I was Super Mom with the perfect store visit. Images of never being able to leave my house flashed through my mind. This was my chance to get out, to prove to myself that I could do it. The caring clerk offered to keep my cart in the refrigerator while I ran home, although not before passing judgment about how I was NOT Super Mom.

Seriously, putting my cart in the fridge was not an option. Buckling, unbuckling, feeding, diapering, pottying ... something would go wrong and then I'd have to do it all over again just to get back to the store to pay for my groceries. What could I do? I was Super Mom and could solve this problem. I decided to call Super Dad. He would fix this. I looked at my phone. No, no, no! It was out of batteries. Who could help me? I pulled my frazzled self together, did some positive self-talk and remembered that I had a phone charger in the car. If I could just call Super Dad, he was sure to rescue me from my misery.

I left the cart filled with groceries and pushed my kid cart out to the car. As I crossed the parking lot, I could see my car but something did not seem right. I opened up the door to the car and wondered why the air conditioning was on. At that moment, my ego slipped to the size of a pea. I had left the car running the ENTIRE time I was in the grocery store. I could not believe this was happening. I stood there in a daze and glanced down at the car floor. There, just under the steering wheel, lay my wallet. I rushed back in the store, paid as quickly as I could and left. On the drive home I was able to regroup and feel proud of my accomplishment. I got a good giggle in and realized that although I was delirious, I had successfully made it out of the house with all three of my children. It's Okay.

Hung-over Horror

Who can blame a mom for wanting to get out and feel alive? After spit up, poop, mess after mess, temper tantrums, etc., isn't a girl due for a night out? I didn't even know if I had the energy to muster up an evening out. But, darn it, I deserved it and I was going to make it happen. I was running on about three hours of sleep and a full day's worth of work, but I was not going to miss this opportunity to get away from the madness and have a night on the town with friends.

Maybe it was the sleep deprivation or the poor eating habits that day, but those beers sure got the best of me quickly. It didn't take long before the laughs and stories were flowing. I had an awesome night. I felt on top of the world. I think I actually felt human again ... not like a worn out moping mommy. I felt so good that it slipped my mind that the following day we'd be in the car for four hours heading to see Great Grandma—oops!

Oops was an understatement. The next morning, not only was I deliriously deprived of sleep, but I was as hung-over as hell. I don't think I had felt that bad since college. The only difference, I didn't have to just care for myself, but my entire family. So, like all good moms do, I tried to suck it up. How bad could a road trip be?

It was the WORST road trip ever. First stop, half hour down the road, one kid had to pee. Second stop, two hours down the road, major baby diaper blowout. Not just a little, on-the-clothes blowout, but an up-the-back, all-over-carrier blowout. Third stop, Great Grandma's and blowout number two (this was just the same as the first). The only problem, I didn't realize blowout number two had occurred until after I carried the kid in and wondered what was all over my sweatshirt.

It might be important to mention that Great Grandma lived in a condo with other great grandparents. The temperature was no cooler than ninety degrees and I might remind you that I was hung-over with poop all over me and all over the car seat cover. My hubby and I tag teamed the kids, the baby and the car seat. Once the car seat cover was in the washing machine, I thought things would turn around. I didn't mind losing my sweatshirt since I was pouring out sweat anyway.

I thought I might be sick. I was SO hot. I made it through lunch, conversation with Grandma and finally switched the laundry so that we could prepare for our trek home. We spent several hours cooped up inside Grandma's two-bedroom condo; anyone with kids knows how this goes. It's a constant broken record. "Don't touch that, get away from there and be quiet!" Oh it was a joy. Grandma was a little leery of why I looked so pale. I assured her I was just fine (secretly wishing away each minute in the heated glass box).

The visit was coming to a close, the car seat cover was clean and put back together, the kids were wound up beyond belief and my headache was still looming. We all got back in the car to make our four-hour trek home. Two hours into the drive, someone had to pee. Lo and behold! There in the baby's car seat was yet another poop explosion.

Lesson learned. Sleep deprived mothers should not have fun. Sleep deprived mothers should not drink. Sleep deprived mothers should just focus on the monotonous daily life tasks to avoid the hung-over hell I experienced. It's Okay.

Ignored

With two kids under the age of two, there were times when I just needed a moment of peace. Occasionally, the oldest one had to get ignored. It was not because I loved her any less, it's just that her needs were not as demanding as those of her newborn baby brother. One time my daughter was reading a book while I was enjoying a quiet moment nursing my newborn son. She was flipping through page after page, shouting, "Mama!" and pointing her finger.

After a while the game got old and I got tired of paying attention to every object she found in her books. Without looking up I began just saying, "Crazy!" and giggled every time she said my name. I was hoping this would satisfy her enough to just keep her reading and give me my moment. After a few more dramatic "Mama's," I realized that she was pointing at her finger. I again ignored, since most of her dramatic mama stories weren't really dramatic at all. I have no idea how it all transpired but, a few minutes later I realized that there were spots of blood all over the book she had been reading.

I finished nursing the baby and decided I should find out what the drama was really all about. Apparently, while looking through books my daughter got a paper cut. A pretty significant one at that! I had to wipe up the blood spill, clean up my daughter's finger and even get a

Band-Aid. All for a little paper cut, that wasn't so little. After all was said and done, my daughter held her finger up, so proud, and shouted, "Crazy!" with a few giggles after. "Crazy!" is now the word in our house that means an injury has occurred. Because I ignored my child, while trying to have a little peace, we don't use the word ouchy or booboo … it's straight to "Crazy!" It's Okay.

Crowded Crib

Oh, my redhead! She is a fun, fantastic and fiery little girl. From day one, her red hair sparkled, shined and got her just about anything she wanted. While we adore our little angel, sleeping has not always been her strong suit. She's not easily fooled and definitely likes things her way. So, when she didn't want to sleep, she didn't want to sleep. Or, when she wanted to sleep a certain way, there was no other way she was going to sleep. Period! End of story. Her way or the highway!

Effort! Lots of effort is what we had always put into getting our girl to sleep. For a while DD batteries did the trick. Oh, did we buy batteries. The swing was on full tilt ALL NIGHT, EVERY NIGHT for SIX MONTHS! Oh, the batteries. All those batteries were bought just to hopefully get a three-hour chunk of sleeping time for us.

After moving on from the swing, there were the late night and early morning drives. I vaguely remember the morning I was desperate to get some sleep after being up all night. I ventured out at four o'clock in the morning, in my robe, praying she would fall asleep, so I could at least get a few hours of rest. I may have run that darn stop sign, "But really officer, I just got her to sleep!"

While the car trick worked for a while, she soon caught on to why we were getting in the car and began to fight that sleep method as well. It was then that I did the unimaginable; at least that's what I thought at the time. I didn't realize the sleep issues would continue. I allowed my daughter into bed with me to watch a DVD, willing her with every passing cartoon character to fall asleep. Once asleep, I would slide her, ever so carefully, off the bed and into her crib. Of course, there were also those nights I was too tired to even do that and allowed those cartoon characters to put me to sleep as well.

I wouldn't have thought it could get worse, but as my fiery red head grew, so did her smart little brain. She knew all our methods to 'trick' her into sleeping. It became so bad that we did the ultimate. We slept with her. IN HER CRIB!

Sadly, either my husband or I would climb into that child-sized bed and lay with our daughter until she fell asleep. Then, trying to be graceful (if an adult can be when climbing out of a crib), we would get out with prayers that she would sleep through the night. You might be thinking this was a tad pathetic. But, hey, it worked. She slept. We could sleep. All was right in the world again. It's Okay.

Money Mat

My daughter was grumpy for about the first four months of her life. If she wasn't being held, she was fussing or crying. She got the nickname, "Grumpopotamus" from me and my husband. She wouldn't nap unless she was held or in the baby carrier. Early afternoon to late evening seemed to be the worst part of her unruly unhappiness. I would wear her around the house, walking laps around the kitchen island until she would finally give up the battle of hating life and fall asleep.

This seemed to be a great weight loss plan, but after four long months of wearing her around, my legs and back began to cause me a considerable amount of discomfort. My solution for this leg and back pain (besides finding a new home for my cranky kid) was to buy a fancy, ergonomic floor mat for the kitchen. Not some regular old carpet square or oval, but one of those gel mats that cashiers get to stand on. While this mat cost that of a second mortgage, it was amazing. Once she fell asleep, I could stand in the kitchen (she, of course, was still strapped to me) with my laptop on the counter and get work done. I felt human again.

The floor mat was one of many impulse purchases I made in an attempt to make parenting easier. If there is one thing I learned from my little Grumpopotamus, it's that you just have to survive. Survival might even mean making a late-night trip to the store to buy an expensive mat for the kitchen. It's Okay.

Rules Schmules

We tried for two years to conceive our second child. We had one bouncing boy and our dream of being a family of four seem to be dwindling away with time. As year three crept by and we still had not become pregnant, I realized I could not look in the mirror without trying every possible option. Adoption crossed our mind, but in the end the aid of fertility drugs brought us a successful second pregnancy. Our perfect family would be complete. I could rest easy and be happy again.

Our second child, however, complicated our world. Being a working parent and dealing with a second child that was not a good sleeper or eater or a happy baby was more than I could manage some days. This was our miracle baby, right? Why, then, did I find myself stressed and regretting our decision to have a second child? I felt guilty that I wasn't spending enough time with our older child because I was exhausted from working and having a new baby. This is the point in my parenting journey that I broke all the standards of great parenting I had set for myself before knowing the challenges of having multiple children.

I let our colicky baby sleep in our bed, with the hope that at least one of us would get some rest. We co-slept for the next two years, our little miracle wedged between my husband and me. As this little thing continued to grow, there were moments that I felt like he was anything but a miracle. More like a monster some days (I say this with the utmost love for him)! I tried every strategy the books suggested, even stripping his room of all toys. I felt that there was no battle I could win. The kid had me cooking ONLY items of food he would want for dinner. Battle after battle … I felt that I didn't have it in me to fight some days.

All these years of going against everything I believed was good parenting caused me to lose belief in my ability as a mother. Why couldn't I do it? Why didn't I have it in me to hold true to the standards I had once set for myself? I hid my feelings from everyone because I was ashamed that I tried so hard for this baby and now my perfect family was anything but perfect. All my standards, all the things I said I'd never do, all my parenting principles—down the drain.

It wasn't until years later and finally some sleep-filled nights that I realized as a parent I was going to break a few rules. You're not a real or true parent until you mess-up. A mom that eats boxed mac and cheese for dinner, sleeps with a toddler, wears a pony tail to work every day … is a real mom. A real mom cannot and should not have it together all the time. I wouldn't trade my boys for anything in the world, nor will I ever give up the parenting battle that continues to challenge me daily. It's Okay.

Closet Space

My baby slept in our closet. Yes, my baby slept in our *closet*! Funny thing is it wasn't for a night or two. It was for SIX MONTHS, and quite possibly longer, though time really blurred together at that point in my life. For six months our closet (granted, you can walk into this closet) was a fourth bedroom upstairs. Having three kids and two adults in three bedrooms shouldn't have been all that difficult. In the olden days, seven to ten kids shared a one-bedroom house with their parents. How could we have been so pathetic to not even be able to manage with three kids in two bedrooms and us in our bedroom?

Our third baby slept in our bedroom in the bassinet for several months. This was perfect; baby in our room and each of our other two toddlers in their own separate bedrooms. Sleep was actually occurring in our house. It was amazing. Having three kids that were three years of age and under was a challenge during the day, so getting a little rest at night was imperative just to survive the daily struggles. It was working.

When our precious third baby got too big for the bassinet, it was time to transition her to the crib. Sleep no longer occurred in our house. When the baby woke up to feed in the night, so did both toddlers. Getting two kids back to sleep, while trying to nurse a third, knowing that both my husband and I had to be up in a few hours ready to function for work, was not the best scenario. Something had to give. In our defense, we tried for weeks to make this situation work, but it just wouldn't. Night after night, putting kids back to bed left us both exhausted, crabby and at our wits' end.

So, we did what all sane parents would do and we made another bedroom. I mean, at least it wasn't the bathroom or something. We set up a pack and play in our closet and that became our third child's bedroom. We could have cared less that we couldn't get to our clothes or shoes. If we didn't prepare the night before and climb over the make-shift crib in our closet, we were out of luck for the morning. But, hey, the house was somewhat restful again. The toddlers were sleeping, the baby was only getting up once and mom and dad could once again rest easy that all three kids were not going to be up and screaming in the middle of the night. It's Okay.

Diaper Disaster

I don't mean to brag, but I am pretty wonderful in the kitchen. It brings me joy to cook for others and it warms my heart to watch them devour the delicious food that I conjure up. So, the day we headed off with our two little ones to a family reunion on my husband's side of the family, I was delighted. The kids were dressed to the nines, looking as beautiful as ever. I had my two side dishes perfectly prepared and I walked into the reunion feeling like Super Mom! This was a great feeling since most days I didn't feel like Super Mom at all—lacking my cape, enough sleep and enough time to get everything in my life accomplished.

My kids were the youngest of the cousins so I didn't worry when I shipped them off with older playmates while I enjoyed some adult conversation. After about an hour, I thought it best to peek in and make sure everyone was still doing okay. When I walked into the room, I noticed a few foul looking puddles on the floor. Quickly, I walked back into the kitchen, trying not to seem too judgmental and made an announcement. "Um, I think one of the kids threw up."

The moms all headed in to see whose kid had done the deed. As we questioned the kids and started to clean up the mess, one of the moms looked puzzled. "I don't think this is vomit. I think it might be poop." In my mind I was utterly disgusted. Seriously, which one of these older kids didn't make it to the bathroom? I decided I should help figure out the puzzle, so I checked both my kids (knowing deep down it really wasn't either of them).

Lo and behold, as I lifted the dress of my youngest daughter, there was a bare bum. She was completely diaper-*less*. Oh my. This mess was from MY KID. In my haste of bringing in my perfectly prepared dishes, I must have forgotten to put a diaper on her. My husband was anything but helpful. "How do you forget to put a diaper on a one-year-old?" I think he proceeded with additional unsupportive comments. The last jab he threw was the best. "Who does that?"

Well, my food was the hit of the day and my diaper disaster was comedy relief for everyone. I was mortified as I cleaned up the mess created by my own daughter. Technically the mess was created by her mother, me, who FORGOT to put a diaper on! I suppose I can't do it all. Super Mom can cook; it's just the minor details of life that go by the wayside occasionally when I am juggling a million things. It's Okay.

Darling Drop

My baby wouldn't sleep. Right from the very beginning he was so different. That second child of mine was NOTHING like the first. I thought having a second child was supposed to be easier because you had done it all before; how wrong was I? My little baby boy was so precious and sweet during the day, but I was far less fond of him at night. He was a baby that NEVER slept!

Not only did my child not sleep, but he refused to ever use a pacifier. Instead, he wanted to get up every hour, on the hour, to nurse himself back to sleep. My mothering skills were getting a workout to say the least. I was exhausted and no good to anyone during the day. My poor first child learned to be very independent during that time and I tried to learn how to survive with no rest.

When he was about two months old I was up in the middle of the night, for the third time, nursing him. I was so tired that I kept dozing off while he was eating. I guess I fell asleep harder than I thought and woke up just in time to grab him by the ankle before he hit the floor! Talk about not sleeping. I didn't sleep a wink the rest of that night; visions of my brain-damaged newborn flooded my brain. I kept imagining how I would explain the drop to my doctor.

That night I vowed to never close my eyes again while feeding him. It was very scary and only added to the sleep-deprived stress I was already under. I don't know how we both survived those sleepless months, but we did. Years later, I can't get the kid to get out of bed in the morning and his nights are restful as ever. If only I could have known then that those moments would pass. Thank goodness for good sleep now. It's Okay.

CHAPTER VI

So Little … So Wise

These little creatures that we call our children grow their 'smarts' much too quickly. It is sad how often parents are proven wrong by their little ones. Most days it's so infuriating, we don't want to admit when they are right. How do they figure things out? Why can't we get away with little white lies occasionally? What happened to the good old fashioned waiting until they are old enough to understand certain things?

When little people say things so profound that we are shocked as parents, why isn't there a manual as to how to handle the situation? Where's the book that gives the step-by-step on answering the questions these kids come up with; from, "Where do babies come from," to, "How is the doctor going to get that baby out of you?" They question heaven and people's intentions and health and, and, and! They never stop. Then of course they have an answer for everything. Many times their answers are so right on, in their own child-like way, that it makes us question our own thinking.

We are taught from a very young age that to not say certain things about people in front of them is polite. But, when these little people question why they can't say the truth, how are we to answer? Yes, the truth hurts sometimes. But, isn't that one of the reasons why our society has become so scattered? No one wants to say the truth. Everyone feels the need to be politically correct. We don't want to expose children to things too early. Why? Why not live in this child-like world? Where things are how they are. Children don't live in the shade of gray that we do as adults, they simply take life for how it is.

Wouldn't that be something; living life through the eyes of a child? It seems that life might be a little more enjoyable. We might actually stop sprinting through life long enough to smell the roses. We might be spontaneous and not miss a moment enjoying the park with friends. We might actually be more productive at work if we'd take time to laugh with those around us. These little people sure are small, but their actions and words are sometimes larger than life!

"Mommy, I Shared!"

So, I was at the hospital giving birth to my second child. My dear friend was watching my one-and-a-half-year-old while I was plenty busy in the delivery room. As a special treat, my friend took my son to buy the best possible gift ever. Stickers! Not just a little pack of stickers, but a gigantic bag full of big stickers. There were ball stickers and star stickers and endless shapes of fun.

The stickers were a big hit for the days that followed my return from the hospital. I was so thankful that my little guy could entertain himself for hours at a time. It was truly a blessing. Being home with two kids was definitely different than just having the one. While he was busy, I could focus on the baby and keeping our life going in an organized fashion.

Fast forward to several weeks after our baby girl arrived. I was cooking dinner and my boy was yet again occupied with the stickers. I made a mental note to go out and buy another bag of those silly sticky wonders. Who knew they would be such a life saver?

My little lady was swaddled up tight and in her bouncy seat on top of the table. While I was turned around preparing dinner, my ever-so-busy sticker boy had helped himself to the top of the table right next to her and started 'sharing' his stickers with his sister. When I turned to check in on the sticker-ing he was doing, I found my swaddled baby COVERED in stickers. All those balls and stars and other shapes were now decorations on my newborn baby's head, face and blanket.

Keeping my cool, I calmly asked my boy what he was doing. With the proudest smile I could ever imagine from a one-and-a-half-year-old he said, "Mommy, I shared!" It's Okay.

"Mom, It's *Not* A Bummer, It's A Boo-Boo!"

What do you say to a kid who is constantly getting hurt? You can only kiss every inch of her body so many times. I wanted to say toughen up or suck it up, but instead I found a one-liner that seemed to do the trick for a while. Whenever my little clumsy monkey fell down and got a 'boo-boo,' I would simply say, "Awe, that's a bummer." I would put on my sad face and move right along to something else. This actually seemed to distract her for a week or two.

Then, as the days wore on and her 'boo-boos' piled up, she got tired of my response. My one-liner was no longer going to work. She fell one afternoon and bumped her knee. Sadly she announced, "Mommy, I have a boo-boo!"

My response was ever so unsympathetic. "That's a bummer."

Angry now, she protested. "Mom, it's NOT a bummer, it's a boo-boo!"

So much for a distraction—she wanted sympathy and was not going to settle for anything less. She wanted attention and she wanted it then and there. Moments later, when her milk plummeted off the couch, her words could not be left without a response. "Oh shit! Oh shit! Oh shit!"

Why do they hear the things they want and ignore all the rest? My ever so smart two-year-old mocked my sailor mouth and then waited to see if **that** would get the reaction she wanted. If only I could know what was going on in that little brain of hers. I guess I should have been saying "bummer" for more things than just the boo-boos. It's Okay.

"Maybe We Should Go To Get-Along-Class Or Something!"

I was done. I couldn't do this parenting thing anymore with my then three-year-old. Not even for a second. It seemed if I said go, she would stop. If I said sure, she'd say never mind. If I offered to help, she could do it herself. If I talked nice, she wanted to know why I was mad. It was constant. She said she loved me, but did everything I asked her not to. When I'd pick her up from daycare, I was greeted by whining, kicking and temper tantrums. Seriously, I could not win with this rotten child and I was done, done, done!

This too shall pass, this too shall pass, this too shall pass. My mantra for positive thinking was not working. The phase was not passing. So, one day I decided to talk to my three-year-old just like I would a grown up. Maybe she could shed light on her manic behavior. Maybe she would have the answers as to why she defied my every word.

Our conversation went like this.

Me: "Honey, we've been having a really hard time getting along lately. Have you noticed this?"

Her: "Yes."

Me: "Well, I am feeling REALLY frustrated and I am not sure what to do. I don't think I can keep fighting like this for very much longer."

After sticking her tongue out at me and mocking me with a shaking head, she continued.

Her: "Well, I'm mad at you."

Me: "Do you like being mad at me and getting in trouble all the time?"

Long pause with an angry face.

Her: "No."

Me: "So, what do you think we should do about this?"

Long pause.

Her: "Maybe we should go to a get-along-class or something."

Sweet smile (seriously, from Dr. Jekyll to Mr. Hyde in .02 seconds)!

Me: "A get-along-class? What would we do there?"

By then she was totally engaged and enjoying the conversation.

Her: "You know, practice being nice to each other."

Me: "Where would we do this class?"

Long pause. She was trying to see how she could make this to her benefit.

Her: "Me and you could go someplace one night, like a restaurant or something and talk about doing and saying nice things."

Me: "So, like I would take you out for dinner and we could have fun together and you think *that* might help us get along better."

Her: "Sure, when are we going? How about we go to McDonalds tonight?"

I don't know where this little thought came from, but it really wasn't a bad idea. Maybe she was feeling left out and like we didn't have time with just the two of us. Obviously she could not verbalize all that to me, but this get-along-class seemed like a pretty good idea. I realized that while she was driving me crazy and not being the friendliest daughter, I wasn't being the kindest mother. So, our adult conversation actually went somewhere and my daughter definitely knew what was needed to mend our fanatic phase of fighting. It's Okay.

"Mom, Please Don't Eat My Snack While I'm In Bed."

What parent hasn't eaten their child's snack when they weren't looking or when they were in bed? Okay, maybe some people have better restraint than I do, but cut a mother some slack. Getting pregnant and fat is not easy and then trying to recover from all that can be just awful, miserable and can cause you to do just about anything.

It all started when my husband and I went on a weight loss kick after baby number two came along. We decided, and rightfully so, that with two children we needed to increase our health to be around as long as we could for our two children. So there were no more snacks, no more fast food and no more comfort. It worked great. We both lost over 50 pounds and felt fantastic. The key was to keep the junk out of the house and not go out and buy it when we felt like we needed it.

Well, as with most weight loss stories, the hardest part is keeping the weight off. Around the time that our first child hit two-and-a-half and our second child was one, yummy snacks started miraculously appearing. From birthday parties to holidays to people just sharing with the cute little kids; we had snacks. But, these snacks were for the kids, right? Wrong! I indulged and loved every minute of it. It was shortly after that point that I became pregnant with our third child.

With the hormones flowing and the snacks continuing to pile up, I couldn't resist. My children unfortunately caught on to my 'sneaking' their snacks. Those who say children are smarter than you think are absolutely right. I'd get caught in the middle of the day sneaking snacks here and there. It was time to out-smart my children. The snacking was saved for after bedtime. It was then that I truly enjoyed things that were terrible for me. But, oh, did they taste good.

Things were moving right along. Weight was piling up, but, hey, I was pregnant. That was supposed to happen, right? Well, shortly after my third child was born, the weight wasn't supposed to continue to increase anymore. I tried to get back on track and again, and the only snacks in the house were those of the kiddos. I tried to resist their snacks. Knowing the snacks weren't good for me and weren't even mine.

I'm weak. I couldn't resist. I continued to sneak their snacks, still mostly indulging at night. One late evening, my ever-so-smart three-year-old came down the stairs. He was supposed to be in bed, so my irritation was very obvious. My tune quickly changed after he began to speak.

That day a friend had made these delicious mouth-watering sugar cookies. The frosting was to die for. There were only two left, one for each child. His eyes drooped, the sides of his mouth hung down and his words were very sincere. "Mommy, please don't eat my snack after I go to bed." I tried to convince him that something like that would never happen. His only response, "But, you always eat our snacks at night and there's nothing left in the morning."

Caught 100% caught by my three-year-old. I resisted my urge to eat those last two cookies and have since tried to find new ways to indulge in sweet treats (or at least cover my tracks better). It's Okay.

"Mom, What Were You And Dad Doing In The Closet?"

The books all say how important it is to foster your relationship with your spouse. They stress how you must communicate and stay intimate. When we were pregnant with our first child, the thought of losing what it was like to be 'kid-less' didn't quite sink in. After surviving pregnancy and a tough few months with our new little one, we got back into a groove and felt like we were doing pretty well.

Then the monotony of life set in and life was tiring. After two more kids, it became difficult to find time to be alone. One of us usually fell asleep on the couch at night while the other one of us slept in the bed comfortably alone. We were also trying to get one of us up and out the door in the morning to get a workout in. The stories you hear from friends about losing time together to be intimate came true for us.

As time went on and the kids grew, we realized that we had to find creative ways to be alone. One particular afternoon, we got the kids busy playing in the tub. They'd get busy playing in the water and sometimes we could get almost an hour of time to tidy things up, get dinner on or just find time to ourselves. That afternoon, we decided to sneak away to the closet; to seize the moment. We needed some fun and the time finally permitted. We used no excuses. Our house had very few locks, but one specific closet was actually lockable. Perfect … right?

Fast forward to the end of tub-time; "Mom, what were you and dad doing in the closet while we were in the bathtub?" Man, we thought we were so sly. We were so proud that we seized the moment and took advantage of our precious little time together alone. Bummer! Caught! Oh well, worth every lie to cover it up. It's Okay.

"Mom, Is This A Special Wipe Or Something?"

So being the mom of two precious girls has its amazing moments. However, it also has its challenges. Both my husband and I work full time and we have tried ever so hard to stay true to who we were before we had kids. We were lucky to have many years of marriage with just the two of us. We always enjoyed going out with friends and relished our beverages. Not that our two kids have hindered our good times, but the good times have changed. It's hard to find sitters every time we want to go out, but we know how important our marriage is and still try to find time together.

Being intimate is something we like to joke about with our friends. 'The Window' has become the reference we use for sex when out drinking with friends. The window is either open for a good night or closed for a night of early rest. My husband has a tendency to say inappropriate things at inappropriate times. While I still think other husbands that make crude jokes are hilarious, my husband's comments have become far less funny as the years have worn on. On nights when we've been out and my husband speaks the wrong words at the wrong times, I've given him *the look*. Then one of our friends will comment. "Oops, I guess the window is closed for tonight!" It really has been quite humorous as this 'window' joke truly opens up the conversation for what *really* happens with intimacy and marriage.

There are always excuses for not being intimate with your spouse. These excuses range from being too tired, to not having enough time, to the kids being awake, to having to get up early. The excuses never end. But, intimacy is important to keep a marriage healthy and after all these years, we still put forth a lot of effort in this area.

Enter my three-year-old and her wonderful questions. Sometimes I am thankful for her curiosity and questioning and other times, I am just stumped. One particular morning, I was stumped.

'The Window' seemed wide open the night before. We were out with friends, had a wonderful time and were looking forward to our own time when we got home. The moment was finally right. Then the crying began. Our youngest had a fever and I was up for the next few hours taking care of the newest ailment. The window got closed, but apparently not before the wrapped condom got put back in the drawer.

My husband headed off to work early the next day, even though it was a weekend (that's another story), and I was left to tend to the kids while feeling exhausted. As I was preparing a fancy Saturday morning breakfast of cold cereal, my three-year-old approached me with something in her hand. I didn't think much of it. Soon she was standing at my side, holding the package out in front of her. "Mom, I found this on the table by your bed. Is it some special wipe or something?" Seriously? I was busy tending to the sick kid and he couldn't even muster up the energy to put the condom back in the drawer? Ugh, window closed for the next month! It's Okay.

"There Are A Lot Of Kids Who Say Naughty Words At School!"

I used to think that sending my kids to daycare would be the hardest thing I'd have to do. That is until I had to send them off to school. We had always used a home daycare and knew the provider well. The children who were at the daycare were always the same and we made an effort to know the parents as well. It was easy to stay on top of what they did during the day, any problems that occurred and exposure to negative words and actions were limited. The big bad world of elementary school was scarier than I thought. I realized that they had seven hours to be exposed to children I didn't know and to interact with adults that I might never have a chance to visit with.

Sending them off to school was a challenge. It felt like they were going off to college and we would never see them again. I never knew if someone would be tender to them when they got hurt or take time to listen to their needs. It was also more difficult to correct their mistakes because so often we didn't know what mistakes they were making. Feeling this way left us very interested when a conversation sparked one night in the car.

At the time, our two children were in second grade and first grade. We were preparing to drop them off at their cousin's house and were going through reminders of dos and don'ts. One of the don'ts was language. We reminded them that even if other children were using inappropriate language, it didn't mean that just because we weren't there, they could use naughty words. It was then that my son piped up. "Well, kids at school say 'bad' things all the time." The conversation that followed went something like this.

Mom: "Really. What kind of 'bad' words are being used? You mean cuss words?"

Son: "I don't know. I don't really want to say. What are cuss words?"

Dad: "Cuss words are naughty words that you can get in big trouble for saying. If kids aren't using nice words, we should know about it."

Daughter: "A lot of times, kids just use the first letter of bad words."

Mom: "So give me an example."

Daughter: "Like the 'b' word."

Mom: "**The 'b' word**. Who in your class is using *that* word?"

Daughter: "Lots of kids use that word."

Son: "What's the 'b' word?"

Daughter (in a whisper, so not to get in trouble): "Butt."

My husband and I looked at each other at this point and smirked.

Mom: "So what other words do they use?"

Daughter: "The 'sh' word."

Son: "What's the 'sh' word?"

Daughter: "Shut up!"

We were totally amused and wanted more.

Dad: "So what other bad words are people using?"

Son: "Well, kids in my class use the 'f' word."

Mom: "**The 'f' word!** Does your teacher know?"

Daughter: "What's the 'f' word?"

Son: "You know, fart."

Now we were nearly rolling in the front seat.

Daughter: "Well, there's also the 's' word."

Dad: "Which one is that?"

Daughter: "You know, stupid."

Long story short, we realized that we hadn't done too terrible in the area of language (even though we religiously sing, "I've got my toes in the water, ass in the sand"). My husband and I have messed up a lot as parents, but I guess we have at least refrained from cussing around the kids. Or maybe it's just they haven't figured out when we are cussing around them. The conversation ended with us encouraging them to avoid using those words. We also provided a good reminder that if they got caught at school using those 'cuss' words they would get in **big** trouble. It's Okay.

"I Can Do This Dad, Don't Worry!"

As a parent of four, I found it most challenging to be the same parent for number one as I was for number four. Looking back and being somewhat wiser now, I know that it is not realistic to be the same parent for each child. Each child we had was blessed with different gifts, strengths and of course, challenges. Balancing life or rather, juggling life, was never easy with four children. I tried my hardest to never miss an event, provide a stable home and just be there for my kids in the ways that they each needed.

My wife and I married while in college and struggled through five births. While only four of our children were able to grow and flourish, each of these five experiences created many chapters in our parenting journey. When our oldest daughter was in high school, I had this parenting thing figured out. I was even willing to give free advice to anyone who would listen. As the years passed, I became humbled to know that I was not the one educating and preparing my children, but rather they were educating and raising me. Each of my children taught me valuable lessons in a variety of ways (some more pleasant than others).

By the time my last child headed off to college, I had reached the following conclusions.

a. I did not know ANYTHING about parenting
b. Parenting is a "crap shoot" or pure luck

c. Learning to laugh at yourself will soften the tears
d. Good beverages with friends and family make it all better

When child number one left for college, I drove her 400 miles and helped her move into her room. Numbers two and three slipped considerably from the first drop off and by child number four, she was telling me what needed to be taken care of when she left. "Dad, I got this!" Not only had she had major wrist surgery the day before she left, but she was in a cast up to her elbow, which she was to keep elevated for several days. She got up in the morning, finished packing her car and loaded herself and her fuchsia cast into her '88 Beretta ready to conquer the world.

She was ready, she was prepared and then she was off. I, of course, checked to make sure she had a pillow ready, so she could elevate her right arm while she steered with her left arm, and that she knew where she was going. She assured me and my wife that she could handle the 400 mile drive on her own and would let us know when she arrived. This was, of course, before every child had a cell phone handy to call at each stop along the way and we had to wait the eight hours to receive the call that she had reached her destination.

Parenting seems to have little to do with teaching your kids how to live a purpose-filled life. Rather, it is the children who raise the parents. The rights of passages that occur and are memorable for children are monumental for parents. These passages became the chapters of many parenting bloopers we have finally learned to laugh about with our grown children. It's Okay.

"Dad, I Think I'm Tall Enough To Drink Pop Now!"

So, my husband definitely has his hard limits. These are the few things in our life with kids that he will NOT budge on. One of these is pop. Sometime in his early years of life, he was told that drinking pop could stunt a person's growth. While there are no studies to prove this scientifically, he has his heart set on this fact being true. He was never as tall as he wanted to be, so naturally he blames it on all the soda he was allowed to drink as a child.

When my son was six years old, he had NEVER had pop. Not even a sip. In fact, I don't think he had ever even drunk from a can. My husband took my boy boating one day and the little guy was sitting in the back of the boat with some other kids. The children had all been given canned lemonade. My husband quickly turned when he heard an annoying slurping sound coming from the direction of where his boy was. He was greeted by the inelegant sight of his son slurping lemonade from the can *without* tilting it. His six-year-old was desperately trying to figure out this 'can' thing on his own, but didn't have the tilt and slurp method down. To his father's dismay, the boy ended up with lemonade all down the front of him. The lack of coordination from his son left him mortified. Oh, how I wish I would have been on the boat that day; to see his father get a taste of his own 'pop fanatic' medicine.

My husband has put the fear of God in my children about this pop thing. Professing that it will stunt their growth and they will no longer grow once they give in to this hideous temptation. When my kids go to a birthday party and are asked if they would like pop to drink, they politely decline. I can only imagine their secret terror for all their friends being served this drug of choice. My son once told me about a time his class won a root beer float party. He was so proud to tell me that he had politely declined and opted for just ice cream. He was so sincere in the way he was telling me. It was almost as if to say he felt sorry for his friends who actually partook in the party.

As my son had encountered more and more birthday parties and witnessed more and more of his friends still growing after consuming pop, he started to doubt the fear that had once consumed his brain and heart. He said to his dad one day. "Dad, I think I am tall enough now to drink pop. What do you think?" My husband only laughed and said in the most childish tone. "Fine, go ahead. Drink all the pop you want. You're happy with how tall you are today, great. Enjoy being that tall for the rest of your life. Going to college shouldn't be a problem at all for someone as tall as you!"

Adult temper tantrum was successful. The kid still won't touch pop. Seriously, I guess my husband has his principles. We all have our thing and pop happens to be his. It's not as if my children haven't had other harmful products containing caffeine. Chocolate is a must in our house. Another funny thing, I drink at least two cans of pop a day, and sometimes more. Guess he can't convince me. It's Okay.

"That's Okay, Accidents Happen."

So every parent loves shopping with their kids, right? Well, I don't think I am in the minority when I say that it is not the most enjoyable experience. I had my two-and-a-half-year-old boy, who I might add was at the tail end of his potty training, and my one-year-old daughter. Right when we arrived at Target, I told my boy we should go ahead and try to potty before we got started shopping. My daughter had out-grown her carrier and was sitting in the front of the cart. Not wanting to put an infant on the floor of a bathroom and not wanting to wrestle with the ginormous cart in the main bathroom, we found the family restroom and went in.

My son still needed a bit of help at this stage, so holding my daugh-ter while my son did his thing was not an option. I share these details because I am sure people reading this will say, "Why didn't she just …?" Anyway, we maneuvered ourselves and our cart into the bathroom, did the duty and washed up. I'm leaving out all the annoying details of helping a two-year-old potty in a public restroom while dealing with a one-year-old not wanting to sit in a cart. When exiting the bathroom, my son ran out of the bathroom ahead of me and the cart into the Target store. I started shouting at him to come back, to wait for mom, to not run off, etc. Of course he listened as well as most toddlers do and was running all over since he had free reign and no mother to grab him.

I soon found out that if the cart was two feet wide, the door for this bathroom was no more than two feet and one inch wide. There was barely enough room for the cart to fit through the door. Let me take a break and mention that at this time, my son was really into a 'game' where he would run, run, run, then slide hands-first (Pete Rose style) on the floor and say, "SAFE!" This was the latest and greatest thing for him. So, I was trying to wrestle the shopping cart through the door of the bathroom, wondering why it was so easy to get in and so difficult to get out, and my son was running all over the entrance to Target, sliding at random times and yelling, "SAFE!" With one big push I shoved the cart out over the door jamb and into the Target store.

It was at that unfortunate moment that my son had actually decided to listen to his mother and come back to the bathroom where I was stuck. At the exact time I managed to shove the cart out of the bathroom, my son came sliding. "SAFE," he yelled, with his hands extended out in front of himself and just in front of my cart. If you can imagine, I had a limited view from inside the bathroom and once he slid, I didn't even realize where he was. Then the crying ensued, along with the complaints of how badly his hand hurt. I figured he had just jammed his finger, got a floor burn or that his finger was squashed a little by the cart. I asked him to open and close his fingers to make sure they 'still worked' and to see if anything was broken. I was totally blowing off the fact that he was actually hurt.

What occurred next was definitely NOT what I had expected. The gush of blood that came out of his hand was everywhere. I mean IT WAS EVERYWHERE! Panicking, but oddly cool-headed for the moment, I shouted at the first Target employee that passed. This poor kid couldn't have been more than 17. "YOU, GET ME SOME HELP, NOW!!!!" He looked at me like a deer in headlights, until I told him to get his manager. There was a flurry of people that came to us. The Target manager proved to be the most helpful and he was great with my son. He looked at my boy's bloody hand and helped me stay calm. He even had one of the employees go to the toy aisle and pick out a stuffed animal for each of the kids to keep them happy. The security guard asked if he should call the ambulance. Not knowing how I was going to drive with a screaming, bleeding two-year-old and a probably traumatized one-year-old, I hesitated only briefly. "Yes, I will need an ambulance." My husband was about 45 minutes away, much too far to be of immediate help.

Someone came up and wanted me to sign documents dismissing Target from all liability. She told me I couldn't leave the store without having these papers signed. I told her that I would not sign the papers, not having read them and that I would be happy to take them with me, read them over and send them back to her (which I did). It was absolute craziness, but somehow, by the grace of God, my daughter stayed calm the whole time—I never heard a peep from her. The amazing store manager bandaged the hand, calmed my boy down and even made him laugh. I realized that the situation had settled down enough that I would be okay to drive the three of us to the hospital. I might add what a good thing this was because when the manager asked the security guard to cancel the ambulance, he apparently had been enjoying our little show so much that he never ended up calling for one in the first place.

Anyway, as we were leaving, the manager looked at my son and said, "I'm so sorry this happened to you." My amazing little guy's response, "That's okay, accidents happen." Classic response from my first born! Amidst all the chaos, I beamed with pride. I called the doctor's office, who told me to head to the ER. Then, I called my husband to relay what had happened. The only parts of that conversation I can remember was my husband saying how I should not have called the ambulance, it was too expensive and why was I at the hospital. He was sure the doctor's office could have taken care of it (classic husband of mine … worried about the bottom-line!). My hubby, whose response did not leave me with the same pride as my son's, met us at the hospital and my mother-in-law came to get my daughter. My son's first words to his dad when he arrived were, "Look at my boxing glove!" His hand and all of his fingers were wrapped to his elbow, resembling that of a boxing glove.

My kid loved the X-ray machine—he thought it was really awesome that someone was taking pictures of his bones. I didn't really lose my cool until the stitching actually happened; there were six stiches needed. It was pitiful. My husband and I had to pin my son down while he was screaming and crying, panicked and scared. I might mention that we didn't have the most 'kid-friendly' or kind nurse. But, luckily, all my kid remembers is the snow cone they gave him when he left the hospital. My son still has that stuffed animal; the one the kind Target manager gave him—he named it 'Mr. A.P. the Cow,' after Adrian Peterson.

I learned two very valuable lessons that day in Target.

1. Always use the bathroom before leaving home.
2. Kids are amazing—my son's positive attitude is one for all of us to learn from.

It's Okay.

CHAPTER VII

Sweet Baby, Curious Toddler, Adoring Adolescent ... NOT

When you meet your child for the first time, it's like no other experience in the world. No one can prepare you for the love you feel and the joy that explodes in your heart the moment you look into your baby's eyes. At that moment, you can never imagine that the love you feel for him or her will ever be over-shadowed by the dislike you have for your kid some days. Again, at that moment you can't believe or understand how some parents get so irritated with their children. Looking into those newly opened eyes and smelling that adorable baby scent, you can't fathom how you would ever be upset with that little, perfect being.

Well, let's be honest. There are days that you are NOT going to like your child. There are days when you cannot believe that you are raising your child. There are days when you wish your child could go visit somewhere else while you regroup. The phases or stages or whatever you want to call them that your children go through are not all cake and ice cream. From fussiness to tantrums, back talk to disrespect. Whatever these months upon months of agony are called, there are some downright miserable moments in parenting.

As your children grow and you look back, it's easy to remember the special moments and reminisce about how fast the time has gone. It's even normal to miss the various stages of development (minus the bad parts). But, really, each phase of life that your child goes through has its challenges, its horrendous moments and its awful parts. Just because you struggle through these times doesn't mean you don't appreciate this gift of a child that you have. It just means that you are human!

Many people try to sugar-coat the difficult times. But, some days, there is no way to make light of the hell you feel you are in. And, some months, there is no way to prevent all the frustration you feel inside. Just when you lighten up and things get better, something else comes up. Enjoying the moment is critical in parenting, but, sometimes, it's best to just forget the moment and appreciate the horror of the stage you are in. Remember, *this too shall pass.*

Kangaroo Shoes

There are some things I learned from my children about their childhood well after the time they were grown and living on their own. I suppose some of these things, these stories, could have gone untold. Had this been the case, I might not have known exactly what kind of childhood my children believe they had. It's easier to hear the stories now that I see them all grown and flourishing, but knowing what REALLY happened when I wasn't around still leaves me with a pit in my stomach.

My boy was ALL BOY! He grew up torturing me and his sisters. I remember vividly the day we all went to Christmas mass and he was about one. I had him and his older sisters dressed to the nines and just needed to get through one hour of mass. The mass was almost over, we were headed to communion and things usually move quickly after that point. I had given him his bottle to try to keep him calm for the last fifteen minutes of our hellish hour. As we approached the Alter to receive communion, he got angry about something; the good Lord only knows what pissed him off that time. He ripped his bottle from his mouth and chucked it up on the Alter, probably ten feet from where we stood; only narrowly missing the priest's head. Bottle throwing! That's the kind of boy behavior I am talking about.

When my children were older there were many days they were home alone without a parent. Apparently this is when many of the untold stories occurred. Looking back, and knowing what we know now, we are lucky that there weren't more ER visits when our children were home alone. One particular day, an incident created quite a story that wouldn't or couldn't go years without being told. My oldest daughter was to watch her siblings including two sisters and her seven-year-old brother. The youngest girl was about five, the boy was about seven and her other sister was ten. I was convinced my eldest would have no problem trying to fight back the torture her brother threw at her.

My son had gotten new shoes. You remember the Kangaroo shoes, don't you? Oh, they were the bomb (this was his word, not mine). They were the coolest thing since sliced bread. Since my son went through about five pairs of shoes a year, I decided to spend a little extra money on him and buy the good ones; thinking maybe these would last. Ha! The joke was on me and he proved me so very wrong that day.

The new shoes provided ammunition for my son to taunt his sisters yet again. He was apparently telling them how cool his shoes were, how strong they were and how nothing they could do to his new shoes would ruin them. That's when he found the rusty nail. My boy, so proud, supposedly said to his little sister, "My shoes are so awesome that not even a nail could get through them!" She, of course, did not back down and encouraged him to try. I think I felt her warming smile all the way at work.

That seven-year-old boy of mine set the rusty nail upright in the kitchen. He backed up to the furthest counter, so he could gain plenty of speed, and ran full blast up to that nail. The leap, I am told, was one of the best the girls had seen. His aim was pretty spectacular, too. He landed right on top of that nail. Unfortunately, he misjudged his new shoes. He underestimated the strength of the old rusty nail to the sole of his Kangaroos. That nail went right through! It didn't just go through his shoes, but right through the bottom of his foot.

I suppose I am glad I wasn't home that day. While his sisters should have felt sorry for him, they didn't. They gained an uncanny amount of satisfaction watching their brother suffer from his own torture! He begged and pleaded for them not to tell mom. However, it was pretty difficult for him to hide the gaping hole that was now open on the bottom of his foot. The tetanus shot he had to receive was a painful reminder that he was not invincible. I'd like to say that he lived and learned that day to settle down and leave his sisters alone, but alas, the tormenting continued to provide additional stories for years to come. It's Okay.

Sneaking Around

I may be old and gray now, but I was sharp as a tack when my kid-dos were young. They didn't think I knew anything, but time and time again, I proved them wrong. Having nine children allowed me to experience just about every possible scenario of parenting. While I wouldn't trade our time with our children for the world, there were moments I wanted to trade them in for more responsible versions.

We raised our children in a small, conservative community. Dances and sporting events were the main sources of entertainment. The wedding dances provided activities for the entire town; even if you didn't know who was getting married. My husband and I allowed our children to have plenty of freedoms, but there were also plenty of rules. These rules were hard and fast and very rarely (to my knowledge) did these rules not get followed. When they weren't followed, there was you-know-what to pay!

One of my girls was a little on the wild side. I knew she liked to have her fun and couldn't always be trusted alone. If there was ever a dance that she did not have a date for, we had a rule that she had to come home with her older, more trust-worthy brother. No exceptions. Well, my children were still children, even though they were teens, and they tried to bend this rule. They tried, but did not succeed.

My two darling teenagers devised a plan to break this little rule of ours. Apparently, if my daughter got 'picked up' at the dance by a good looking teenaged boy, my ever so trust-worthy son would meet up with her around the block so they could pretend like they had been together the whole time. This reuniting may have happened several times before I caught on, but as all good mothers do, I figured them out.

On this particular evening, my son arrived early or my daughter arrived late for the reuniting. When I spotted my son, you could see the fear in his eyes. While I was not usually up this late, the 'look' was worth every hour of sleep I missed. It was as if he was saying, "Oh dear Lord, what is MOTHER doing up and in the yard? I'm in deep doo-doo!" My words were anything but sweet and my tone was anything but gentle. "Where's your sister?" Again, if I wasn't seething, I would have found sheer enjoyment watching my ever so responsible son squirm with every lying word. "She's coming," he said, so timidly.

My son jetted inside; I'm sure to try to send off smoke signals to warn his late sister that I was awake, but he was too late. I had headed in to await the arrival of my troubled teen. Seconds later, my sweet little teenaged rule-breaker had her shoes off, one in each hand and was attempting to tip toe up to her room. Ha! She was caught in the act. I almost wanted to laugh at her shock to see me as well. My booming voice could be heard throughout the house. It was then that I heard the snickers out of the son I thought I had so sternly scolded and taught a lesson to. How dare him. "You quit your laughing and go to bed!"

While this was just one incident among many, my husband and I couldn't have been more proud of our nine children. Each phase brought new challenges, new laughs and certainly new rules. I will never forget the many times our rule-breakers got caught and the priceless looks they had thinking they outsmarted us. Darn kids. It's Okay.

Locked Out

Having a car with On-Star definitely has its benefits. Especially when your two-year-old son locks you out of the car and then laughs! My oldest was in preschool that year so there were always two pick-ups late in the day. On this particular day, I was exhausted. Our baby was still not sleeping through the night and work had gotten the better of me. Visions of the fast food I was going to pick up for dinner and a night of TV watching on our comfortable couch danced in my head.

First stop, daycare to pick up my two-year-old and my baby. It should have been quick and easy, but it was NOT. The fit I had to deal with leaving the daycare was enough to make me want to sit on the curb and let someone else claim my kids. While the baby was actually asleep in the car seat, I knew this was not the time of day I needed her to be sleeping. We managed to fight through the tantrum to get to the car. I had the baby seat in one hand and the kicking, screaming two-year-old in the other. I just needed to get this terrible two-year-old in the five-point harness car seat and all would be fine. We could get to preschool and still make it home to enjoy my visions.

I set down the maniac for two seconds, just long enough to click the baby carrier into the base. It was in those two seconds that my life continued to spiral downhill. The two-year-old jetted to the front seat, where the keys sat ever so beautifully in the cup holder. I went around to the front of the car, on the driver's side. I knew he was going to play NASCAR. It was then that I heard the distinct sound of the car locking. No! No, no, no!

"Unlock this door! Unlock this door right now!" Yeah, right. The only person who cared what I was screaming about was the neighbor looking out his window laughing at me. So, now, my buck-led-up baby and my two-year-old, along with my keys, were locked in the car. Some might assume that he didn't know how to unlock the car and that was why he ignored my requests, but it was just pure defiance.

It was sheer luck that I had my cell phone in my pocket that day. It saved my pride from having to go back into the daycare, ask to use the phone and admit that I had absolutely zero control of my son. I called On-Star and told a little white lie. This lie was told to salvage any remaining self-worth I had that day. I told the nice man I talked to on the phone that my dog was locked in the car. I suppose my son was act-ing somewhat like a dog that day. Anyway, I asked if he might be able to speed along the process of unlocking the car doors so my sweet little poodle could get some air.

That night was as far from my dancing visions as possible. I was still fuming by the time I got to preschool to pick up my oldest child and I was too emotionally drained to even drive through a fast food joint on my way home. My son's craziness nowhere near ended until well after he went to bed, so my couch didn't even see my bottom until 8:00 pm. The silver lining to all this; boy was I glad I paid for my On-Star that month. We religiously kept that extra amenity handy for many years to come (and a few more 'dog' lies when needed). It's Okay.

Locked In

Change is about the only consistent thing you can count on when raising children. Even though you can count on change, it didn't make encountering it any easier for me and my husband. We were raising a daughter, an 'only child' and unfortunately, she had a particular dislike for change. One specific change and challenge began when our little family of three was offered the opportunity to return to Wisconsin, our home state, following two years of living in the state of Missouri.

Naturally, I assumed that everyone, including our four-year-old, would be excited and ready to head for home. After all, home was where grandma and grandpa, aunts and uncles, friends and the comfort of the familiar all resided (at least to me and my husband, anyway). It seemed like the perfect time to make our journey back to the many things we missed; particularly since our only little angel would be starting kindergarten in the fall. It would be the flawless fresh start; new house, new city, new school, new friends. Everything felt bright and shiny with the expectation of an abundant future ahead.

"Let's roll," I thought. And roll we did, right into an unexpected situation that came at us out of the blue. This situation could be compared to the blowing north winds off Madison, Wisconsin's beautiful lakes. Our little darling did not have the enthusiasm we did over building a new house and living in a condo while we were patiently waiting to move. Nor did she appreciate or understand why we moved in the first place. Despite daily trips to visit the building site of our new home, our daughter showed a distinct apprehension about what this new life was actually about and what her place was in it. Her confusion and irritability about everything changing around her and her inability to understand and communicate her feelings was more than apparent. This resulted in behavior I had never experienced in the past. I was so excited, why wasn't she?

Thinking positively, I hoped that starting school would provide the remedy to what was upsetting our little girl. Unfortunately, once school started, she developed stomach aches, headaches and a general avoidance to anything social; from birthday party invitations to play dates. A visit to the pediatrician revealed that our daughter was fine physically; she just wasn't fine about all the change. I felt like she needed a social intervention and she needed it fast.

As luck would have it in snowy Wisconsin, the blessed event of a 'snow day' came calling, canceling school and dropping mountains of white fun in our neighborhood. It arrived just as I was considering obtaining a professional opinion about our daughters discomfort with her new environment and social adjustment to her new surroundings. No kid can resist the call of pristine white snow and my daughter wouldn't be any exception.

I was thrilled when she climbed into her snow boots and said she wanted to slide down the hill that ran along the side of our lot. My little darling was suited up and ready to hit the slopes just as our doorbell rang. There stood our two adorable neighbor girls, sleds poised behind them. They wanted to know if my daughter would like to sled with them and then have cocoa at their house later. Perfect, social intervention! My daughter peered out from behind me and I could feel her resistance to their invitation mounting without even looking at her. It was obvious that she was ready to go outside, so when she protested with a very firm, "NO," I countered with a very determined, "YES."

The neighbor girls seemed as surprised at my daughter's response as I was. I told them that I needed to talk with her for just a moment and that she would be out shortly. Naturally, the classic battle ensued.

Me: "YES."

Her: "NO."

Me: "Make some friends."

Her: "I don't want to."

Me: "They'll feel hurt if you don't go out."

Her: "I don't care. I'm not going."

Me: "Yes you are."

Finally, desperate for my daughter to make some friends and have some fun, I shoved her out the door and locked it behind her. I walked away feeling sick about what I had just done. What had I just done? I had just locked my five-year-old outside, with no intention of letting her back in the house. Talk about 'forced fun'!

Naturally, I had to check on my daughter's reaction to my sudden decision to send her out into the storm; her storm that is. There she sat on the front step, snow sifting down on the hood of her snowsuit. She was MISERABLE! Now what? I returned to our kitchen, my place of refuge when the chips seemed down. Unable to contain myself and my frustration over my door locking action and my daughter's reaction, I returned to the front door and cautiously pulled back the drapery. No little, pouty girl! This could be good or bad. Just then I heard shrieks, shouts and laughter. I walked to the windows facing the sledding hill on the side of the house. There she was, that fiery girl unwilling to change, sliding down the hill behind one of the neighbor girls. Head back, laughing and catching snow in her mittens on the way down her snow slide. The girls tumbled off the sleds and ran back up the hill exchanging lots of giggles and chatter as they pulled their sleds behind them.

It snowed all afternoon and the girls continued their fun. Finally, dusk was setting in and I was about to call my daughter inside. Just then, the doorbell rang and all three girls stood in front of me looking like little snowmen. My daughter was beaming and asked the question that made my heart sing. "Could you make cocoa for us at OUR house Mom?" That was it! That was the intervention I had hoped for. I knew then that everything was going to be OKAY, changes and all! The future was bright once more. Who would have guessed locking my daughter out of the house was just the intervention she needed? It's Okay.

Morning Madness

My son has always struggled to get ready in the morning and be on time to where he needs to go. ALWAYS! Mornings were usually filled with yelling and threat after empty threat. I kept thinking it wasn't fair that his limitations were making us all suffer. The threats never worked because I never followed through on them. This son of mine, who once struggled as a boy, was now struggling as an adolescent. Surely, he should have gotten better with time (or so I had hoped).

One day, I was tired of yelling. My voice was particularly calm that morning. How, I do not know. But I decided today was the day. No more yelling. No more empty threats. We were leaving. We were leaving ON TIME! My threat came out ever so smoothly to my then twelve-year-old. "If you are not ready on time today, we are leaving without you!"

So, when it was time to go, my daughter and I got into the car and started driving down the street. The guilt started to settle in and I second-guessed myself a little as the van wheels rolled from the drive way into the street. Nope! I had to do this. This was the day. No more empty threats. I paused for only a brief second and decided to keep going.

It was in the next few moments that I think the whole neighborhood was awakened by the sound of my almost teen son. Then I saw him through the rearview mirror, running for dear life, chasing us down. I knew that eventually I would have to stop, but I was determined to make my point. No more late mornings! I kept right on driving.

Unfortunately, my perfectly laid plan was squashed by a little old lady who wanted to save the day. Her honks were heard for miles and her finger nearly dislodged from her hand because she was pointing so hard at me. She was letting me know that I had forgotten my son. Really? Really, you think I don't know that my son is back there, screaming at the top of his lungs and chasing us down like a madman? How embarrassing. Here I was, trying to teach my son a lifelong, valuable lesson and I WAS BEING SCOLDED; scolded by the little old lady who not only honked and pointed, but stared at me with the most disappointing look. Even my Grandmother could not have done it better.

Rotten boy of mine! This was supposed to be about you! I was the only one that looked bad. I wish I could say that this morning ended all morning madness from that day forth. It didn't, and that's provided numerous more stories to be told. It's Okay.

Haircut Hell

Juggling life with my three children is never dull and something I definitely love. This love, however, is present on some days more than others. It does, of course, as anyone will tell you, take a village to make raising children happen. One of the village members helping to support the raising of my children is my fabulous hair stylist. She has bravely and graciously taken on the task of cutting my boys' hair. You might be wondering about my third child. Well, let's just say that I'm not yet at the stage of having a scissors within a two-mile radius of my toddler daughter's beautiful curls.

One particular day I ventured out with all three kiddos to get the boys' hair trimmed. The fiasco that ensued turned out to be more of a disaster than I could have ever imagined. Thank goodness for that village I mentioned.

Our fiasco began with my thirsty four-year-old. While helping himself to a cup of water, he overdid it at the water dispenser, which resulted in his **full** cup of water being spilled all over the floor. Within the next minute, my oldest, a five-year-old, asked the stylist if he could use her scissors to cut off his you-know-what, so that he wouldn't have to go to the bathroom during his haircut. Then, after asking my four-year-old repeatedly if he had to go potty, he finally decided that he did. Upon doing the deed, he came back from the restroom and into the salon area BUCK NAKED, asking me to wipe his butt. While walking back to the bathroom, the same darling managed to stub his toe, which, of course, was followed by screams of bloody murder for the next seven minutes.

Meanwhile, my two-year-old little girl became hysterical, thinking that I had abandoned her while I was helping her brother via said poopy patrol. The cherry on the top to this sweet visit was when we left the salon; I was greeted by a wide open door on my minivan. Apparently, the boys had left the sliding door of the minivan wide open during our *entire* visit.

At the time I was ready to throw up my hands yelling 'serenity now'! I, of course, look back upon this day with grins and chuckles. And thankfully, our lovely hair stylist was a sweetheart about it all. She was kind enough to let me know that our little comedy of errors provided the salon with much needed humor and entertainment for the day.

As you can imagine, EVERYONE in the salon knew our clan after the previous visit. When we walk in, it's as if they expect to be rolling by the time we leave. Rest assured, the comedy troop continued! A subsequent trip to the salon resulted in my little girl asking one of the stylists if she was a Fairy (in my daughter's defense, the stylist did have a short purplish pixie hairstyle and sported lots of colorful tattoos). My middle child then didn't let me down and followed up the embarrassment by asking a woman in the waiting area, with highlighting foils in her hair, what the heck was wrong with her head. The fun never ends. It's Okay.

Painted, Polished and Toothless

Shortly before my daughter's fourth birthday, we welcomed into the world a bouncing baby boy. We were so excited to have a complete family of four. Little did we know, our lives would never be the same. Our life was suddenly more interesting. This bouncing baby boy has kept us on our toes from day one. I'll break it down into just three major catastrophes, but you should know that there were many more and that the Poison Control Center knew me by name.

Catastrophe #1: Spray paint. My 15-month-old spray painted his face. When my son was around 15 months old, he had his first trip to the ER. This was no regular ER visit for stiches or a broken arm. Oh no, this second child of mine would do nothing that was regular. This was downright frightening. The little guy was into everything and after exploring in his Grandpa's garage, he dropped a can of spray paint, only to have it explode in his face. While this is a very long and emotional story, I'll spare you the gory details. Everything turned out okay; that is if you can get past the $2500 ER bill!

Catastrophe #2: Toothless. My two-year-old bundle of joy knocked out his front tooth. When he was two-and-a-half, he was lying on the floor dangling a toy over his face. He dropped the toy and knocked his front tooth loose. It was hanging by a thread. Of course it was Saturday, so we had to call his dentist at home. He met us at the office and we were told he would have to pull the tooth. Seriously, I was mortified. There was no way to salvage the tooth. My little two-year-old boy was toothless. This young man wouldn't be getting permanent teeth for years and I was truly humiliated every time someone asked what happened to his tooth (which occurred daily for about a year).

Catastrophe #3: Polished. My five-year-old found the nail polish! One lazy morning shortly after his fifth birthday (side note ... at this point he was still toothless, but had no remnants of spray paint any longer), my boy came running, rather bounding, into our room with his hand over his eye. My husband and I had not gotten out of bed yet and had both been dozing on and off. We were no longer sleepy after we noticed our son's face was covered in blood. It was dripping everywhere. Our first thought was that he had stabbed something in his eye and he was now going to be a one-eyed, toothless kid. I started screaming hysterically as all the terrible visions raced through my mind. It was then, that my much calmer husband said, "What is that smell?" We realized quickly that our little gem had broken a bottle of red nail polish and rubbed it in his eye. His polished eye kept him from receiving as severe a consequence for the polished shoes, cabinets and carpet.

While these were just three of the catastrophes encountered in our parenting experience, it gives you a little insight about the knowledge our second child imparted on us. We learned about things we could have never imagined. As with most child catastrophes, the results were okay in the end. The spray paint and nail polish didn't do any damage to his eye sight, the paint wore off of his face to give him his original color and his permanent tooth eventually filled the gap he had had in his mouth for years. It turns out that being a snaggle-tooth really suited his personality. The 'in home' care package I received from Poison Control turned out to be very helpful throughout these critical years. Our boy is turning out to be a diamond in the rough, but we wouldn't trade him for any gem in the world! It's Okay.

Motor Mouth

Seriously, will you ever shut up? Those are words we do not allow in our house, but there have been many times I have wanted to shout those very words from the roof top. My kid would NOT STOP TALKING and he was only three years old. This second child seemed behind at the age of one. I remember thinking that, compared to my first child, he was not at the level he should be. He wasn't babbling as much, making as many sounds or saying as many words and sentences.

I really thought I had failed my second child. Things were so busy with a toddler and a baby. I didn't read to my second child as much as my first. I didn't spend as much time talking to him. I felt like my second kid may never make it through school to college because I let him down from day one.

Well, those thoughts of imperfect parenting quickly left my brain when my neglected second child started out-talking our first child. This all happened around the time he turned two. It's not that he was all that advanced, he just had a LOT to say. A LOT! He never stopped. He talked in the car, during meal-time, playing around the house, getting ready for bedtime … he *never* stopped. It was story after story after story. There were days when I didn't think I could listen to his voice for one more second.

I had to survive this struggle somehow. What I really wanted to do was to scream at him to shut up, but that was against every parenting principle I had. So, I tried a new strategy. I just needed some relief. I needed a way to foster his needs and not squash his spirit; but to give my poor ears a break. The new strategy I tried was zoning. If I would give him enough, "uh huhs," or "oh yeahs," he seemed to be satisfied. My needed break was had.

Unfortunately, my motor mouth of a son had other talents aside from just talking. He caught on to my zoning and used it to his benefit. There was a period of time in my parenting when this little guy got me to agree to things I would have never agreed to, had I actually been listening. Candy, play dates, sleeping in the backyard—my strategy got blown. My motor mouth still tells a million and one stories. I'm trying my hardest to listen and to avoid the dreaded words that are not allowed at my house, but some days, I just wish he would *be quiet*! It's Okay.

Not So Perfect

When I was pregnant with my first child, my husband and I decided that I would stay at home. I couldn't wait to spoil my little baby girl with love. All I ever wanted to be in life was a housewife and a mother. I knew that I was going to be the best mom that ever walked the planet. I would show everyone how it was done. Easy as pie, easy as 1, 2, 3! I couldn't wait and knew that I would have nothing to complain about. It was going to be perfect.

So my first imperfect parenting experience happened before my daughter even left the womb. Not only was I more than a week overdue, but I had to endure labor hell to get her out. It took 14 hours of labor and a miserable hospital experience to begin this perfect parenting journey I was so excited about.

Once she was in my arms, I thought the ease of being a mother would fall right in place. Six weeks. It took six weeks for that perfect girl of mine to latch on and feed properly. I realized all too soon that there might be a little more to this whole 'mothering' thing than I had once thought. My perfect stay-at-home-experience was being spoiled by the very thing that allowed me to be at home. My baby! I had this image that breastfeeding would be comforting and adoring, not frustrating and draining.

Our first child really was a wonderful baby and staying at home was something I never regretted. But, it became apparent time and time again, that the picture perfect parenting world DOES NOT exist. I was so proud that my daughter thought I was the best thing in the world, but it was somewhat embarrassing that I couldn't leave her with anyone until she was almost three. This little lady of mine had become so attached to me and **only me** that we were apart only a handful of times, and those times were miserable for the both of us.

After all these years and another baby later, I have learned a great deal. My daughter, who wouldn't latch properly, now eats everything in sight. The same girl who wouldn't leave my side is now a confident and successful ten-year-old who can boss people around just fine. Looking at this girl and my son, it's obvious that they are turning out to be great kids. The small stuff that caused me the most stress in the beginning turned out not to matter as much as I thought it did. While this parenting thing was much more difficult than I had assumed, I have done the best job I could. I have no regrets. Things haven't been perfect, I haven't been perfect, but really, I've done a pretty darn good job. It's Okay.

Head Buster

Second babies are amazing. If nothing else, it's so nice to have done the whole parenting thing before. I knew what to expect and was ready to rock the baby world. Nursing my second child was going great and I actually had a fairly good sleeping baby. Well, my good spirits about my new baby were quickly soured by my two-year-old. The terrible twos had gotten the best of him and the best of me. When my first child was a baby, nursing was a wonderful bonding time for both of us. I could sit and enjoy a comfy chair with a nursing pillow. It was cozy, pleasant and picturesque.

Fast forward to nursing child number two. There was no bonding time during the day. It was like fast food for my second child. The amount of times I had to pull him off my boob to tend to my rotten two-year-old was uncountable. There was no comfy chair or nursing pillow. I was on the floor or propped over the table. Moving while nursing became the common form.

One morning while on maternity leave, I was desperately wishing for my working days. Not because I didn't love being home with my boys, but seriously, I just needed a moment of peace. I needed a moment of feeling like I was more than just a milk factory working on overload, trying to keep up with my desperate consumer. That morning, my two-year-old was extra terrible. Apparently he thought running away from his ever-correcting mommy was funny. I had had it. I was going to show him! I stood up, my baby still hooked on my boob, ready to show him who was boss. I was so focused on the big boom of my two-year-old that I completely missed the big boom that occurred on the door jamb I was passing through. My poor baby got his head whacked in the doorway.

Mom = zero, Terrible Two-Year-Old = million and one! At least we escaped brain damage that day and for the many more head shots that followed! I may have lost a battle that morning, but spent the next few years playing catch-up, bound and determined NOT to let my child beat me. It's Okay.

CHAPTER VIII

Parent Of The Year ...
What's That

O nce again, it is good to be reminded that everyone is the perfect parent, until they actually have children. There is NOT a perfect parent, or a perfect child for that matter, in the world. There certainly are people or kids who are close, but no one is perfect. Pre-children, I knew that I was going to be the best parent. I had lots of knowledge about children and *for sure* knew what was best. Plus, how hard could it really be?

Well, let's just say that my goals for parent of the year shrunk down to parent of month within a few weeks of having my second child. And from there, within another week, I was down to hoping for parent of the week. Then shortly after our third child was born, I strove to get parent of the day. Now, with four children, it's safe to say that if I get parent of the moment, I'm doing a darn good job.

It's not realistic to think we can do it perfectly. We are going to mess up. It's important to realize that you will do something great, only to be followed by three other mistakes that over-shadow the great thing you just did. It's okay. Give it up. The award for *Parent of the Year* doesn't exist. And if it did, whoever did get the award was sure to have screwed up on more than one occasion (but, maybe just didn't admit to it).

Daycare Fever

No, this is not okay. I know this is not okay. But, who hasn't done it? This was what I asked myself that dreadful morning before I pumped my kid with Tylenol and sent her off to daycare with a fever. That morning, I knew I couldn't miss a 9:00 a.m. meeting. It was too late for my educator husband to call and get a substitute. What were we to do? I know I am making excuses, but we were really in a bind.

My thoughts started streaming as I drove off from the daycare that day. What if it's just her teeth? Maybe she just got really hot when she slept. If she has a virus, chances are she got it from daycare or she was already contagious yesterday. Excuse after excuse continued in my mind so that I could justify my actions. How many excuses did I come up with, you might ask? I just had to make it through my meeting. Surely if it was a real issue, the Tylenol would wear off, I'd get the call after my meeting and then I could tend to my little angel.

So, I sent my kid to daycare with a fever. I did the unspeakable and to top it all off, I lost parent of the year **again** that day! I think I had lost it the day before as well; though I can't remember what all I had screwed up on previously. That dreaded fever-filled day was supposed to be my fresh start. It's Okay.

Feeder Fish

Now, mind you, this title does not tell the whole story. Yes, I did kill two of my youngest son's fish, but it was definitely not intentional; and, in my defense, they *were* just feeder fish. You may need a little background so that I can regain some self-worth, some dignity and some pride. I am the mother of three boys, born three years apart. Everything in our house is a competition or a battle. The three of them, each equally full of 'boy' qualities, has made me appreciate our girl dog more than you can imagine, even though she hasn't learned how to clean up her own hair yet.

So, I digress; back to my fish-killing. Imagine a calm, relaxing, peaceful afternoon in a household of five (minus the husband who was busy working on the weekend, leaving me all alone to deal with my three angels). Then, imagine the complete opposite of that serenity, and you'd have my afternoon perfectly pictured. Not only was I trying to get our house put back together after a long week of two full-time working parents and three full-time students, but I was also trying to add in the task of cleaning the fish tanks. You'd think that we could just have one fish tank with three fish, but alas, trying to avoid a battle or competition of whose fish is the best or whose fish can do what, we purchased three fish tanks so each boy could tend to his own fish in its own fish tank, without comparison.

They each had their own fish tank, so each could take responsibility for feeding the fish and cleaning the fish tank, right? Wrong! Mom got the joy of keeping those grimy tanks clean. So unfair, as with most cleaning duties in our house of boys! Anyway, I digress again. I got each of the boy's two fish into three different cups! Two tanks were done when a WWF wrestling match ensued in the room next door. The tank cleaning battle took a brief pause while the wrestling referee (that's me, too) had to break up the tangled mess. Once the wrestling match was over, the cleaning of the tanks and rooms continued.

Somehow, along with the other eight dirty cups that got collected upstairs, the cup with the only two remaining fish in it, ended up in the kitchen downstairs with the other dirties. Again, as a disclaimer, after the wrestling match ended, the Cold War began down in the basement. Keeping up with the boys, while trying to complete tasks, isn't always the easiest thing to do. I tend to get distracted, as most parents with multiple children do! It's nice to joke with other parents in similar homes who have the same struggles, so that I'm not judged as a mom who doesn't have it all together. I am as together as any full-time working mom can be! It's life.

As you can see, I'm still trying to gain back my pride, my self-worth and any amount of dignity I can muster. There, on the counter, with the other million dirty dishes, was a cup full of water including my youngest son's two darling fish; his pride and joy. I had a moment of peace. When these moments come, you work like a tornado to get as much done as possible because following moments of peace are always moments of hell. When working quickly, sometimes the most thorough work does not get complete.

That afternoon, the kitchen was spotless. Every dish clean, every cup washed, every towel folded. The floor even sparkled for a brief minute or two. I actually felt pretty good about my accomplishment. It was at that moment that my accomplishment turned into failure. My little boy came into the kitchen with a confused look on his face. "Mom, where are my fish?"

Well, crap. The pit in my stomach grew larger than a deep gaping hole. Every accomplishment I made that day went down the drain, right along with those two fish. Yes, apparently in my haste to clean the kitchen, when dumping glass after glass of water out, I missed the one with the fish in it. Who can blame a mom for trying to keep up on household duties? Who can blame a mom for doing amazing things sporadically throughout the day in between the child battles constantly occurring? Who? I'll tell you who; that little five-year-old boy of mine, who didn't care what I had accomplished that afternoon. He only cared that there were no more fish in his tank.

Needless to say, we made a trip to the pet store that night, returning home with two new fish for my little man. The kids got to bed late and I lost a few hours of the doctor-recommended sleep. In my defense, those two fish were feeder fish anyway. They were going to have to get eaten up by something; they just probably didn't expect it to be the drain. It's Okay.

Slammed

When my oldest child was almost one, I ventured off to the store. Between work and raising a one-year-old, it was always daunting to get to the store on a regular basis. I was in a rush, wanting time to cook dinner when I finally made it home after a long day. I was already somewhat annoyed with the car next to me that parked within a foot of my car. Thank goodness for mini-van sliding doors or I would have had to climb through the cab of the van to get my one-year-old out the other side.

I set my angered feelings aside and focused on the task at hand. I grabbed my one-year-old, threw him on my hip, slammed the door and took off. My rush was stopped short by the pull of my son's foot still in the door and the agonizing scream of my baby.

Feelings of horror and shame flashed through my mind. So much for mother of the year, I didn't even get it for a day. My son was screaming, I was sobbing and I couldn't even move between the cars. Forget the food; I had to salvage the foot. I immediately took him home and began my motherly examination. He wasn't walking yet, so I couldn't look for trouble with pressure, but the foot definitely, kind of, maybe, looked swollen. I called Children's Hospital and explained the situation and my concerns. I didn't know if he should go in for x-rays or for an amputation. The horrible images of the car door shut on his foot would not leave my mind.

Well, my worry for the foot began to leave my mind ever so quickly as my concern for Child Protective Services (CPS) taking my son away flooded my thoughts. The hospital interrogated me over the phone, thinking I was covering up abusing my son. As if I didn't already feel bad enough. Screw the x-rays, we threw a little ice on the ankle, grabbed some fast food and prayed that his foot would turn out just fine. It's Okay.

Sister Search

When you leave your children with a babysitter, you worry, but you tend to think that things are going to be just fine without you there. That morning as I kissed my kids goodbye and wished them a happy day, I had no idea what was in store. I had no idea that the school would be calling me with the most impossible thing happening.

The babysitter was to take my oldest child to school and then tend to my two younger children at the house. We lived about three blocks from the elementary school and walked in nearly all weather conditions. I didn't realize that my four-year-old knew the route all too well and didn't like the fact that her older sister was leaving her and her baby brother alone with the babysitter.

Apparently the babysitter was preoccupied—or napping, according to my spirited four-year-old. So, my little lady decided that she wanted to 'visit' her sister at school. She walked out the front door, crossed three different intersections, walked into the elementary school and straight for her sister's classroom. Her sister happened to be out at recess, so she proceeded to walk through the school searching for her big sis. I can only imagine my four-year-old perusing the elementary school ALL ALONE and parentless!

Thank heavens she had enough sense not to take her baby brother along for this little excursion. I don't know how long she roamed the building, but eventually she was stopped by one of the teachers at the school. Being the small town that it was, the teacher recognized who she belonged to and questioned her about why she was up at the school. Not too long after that, I got a phone call from the school. Mind you, I still hadn't heard from the babysitter and my guess is that she didn't even know my daughter was missing this whole time (scary … I know!).

Mortified, I left work to pick up my daughter. I tried not to be too angry with that curious child of mine, but she definitely knew she was not supposed to be out and about on her own. Needless to say, I didn't return to work that day. I relieved the babysitter indefinitely and had a long heart-to-heart with my four-year-old about the dangers of the activity she partook in. It's Okay.

Garage Girl

Every year our school district offers a wonderful opportunity a couple days before school begins to meet our children's teachers for the upcoming school year and practice getting to school 'safely' prior to the first day. There are always booths set up with information on the PTO, Girl Scouts, Cub Scouts and a variety of other things. The school also provides a meal consisting of a small hot dog, chips, a drink and a cookie. This is perfect, right? A free dinner for a family of six; our budget likes this.

A problem arose for us because my wife had similar work commitments the same night as the school event. She said she wanted to participate in the annual ritual, but could not stay the entire time. In order to save herself some guilt, she came with us up to school and stayed for about ten minutes; long enough to quickly be introduced to the teachers and to grab the needed paperwork. Paperwork is not really my forte, so it was nice to have her along.

On this occasion, she had a bright idea that we should fully *experience* the school 'safety' opportunity, suggesting that it would be wonderful for the kids and me to walk home from school. Of course, this was such a wonderful idea because she would not be there. The walk is about six blocks through the neighborhood; a good half mile and one that the kids are never pleased about making. She took our car and left me to tend to the kids and to make it 'safely' home! Ha, what wishful thinking!

At the time our oldest was six and going into 1ˢᵗ grade, our second child was five and going into kindergarten, our third child was three and our youngest child was almost four months old. The fun began shortly after my wife departed (again, with the car).

After getting food for the three eaters and me, we sat down at one of the school cafeteria tables in the middle of the playground. It was August and the 90 degree heat was blazing off the playground concrete. Sheer joy occurred as I tried to open chips, squirt ketchup, exchange drinks, exchange cookies, get napkins, get napkins, get napkins and, of course, try to prevent spills. The sweat was starting to drip pretty good at this point. It was probably a blessing that I didn't have a chance to sit down, since I don't know that I could have gotten out of those terrible cafeteria tables. Surely I would have fallen with all the luck I had that evening.

Moments after devouring every speck of food provided by the school, I started to hear, "I'm hungry," out of all three kids. This was my signal that it was time to head for home.

After crossing the main road from the school to the neighborhood we had two choices on which way to go home. I thought it would be 'fun' (I might add that this night was anything but 'fun') to let the kids decide which way to go. They did great deciding to go left. After walking one block we had another choice to make. This was when things started to spiral. Four of us agreed to go right and one of us wanted to go straight. I thought that if I went right the five-year-old would surely see the error in his way and follow. Boy was I mistaken; one of many mistakes I made that night.

I went right, he went straight. After about a half block I realized he was *not* going to follow us. I started to get that sinking feeling in my stomach. I got worried and decided to pick up the pace to meet him at the next corner. Sweat was no longer dripping, but rather pouring down. We made it to the corner and I caught sight of him; he was NOT happy, but he began to follow us. It was my first win of the night.

We proceeded to walk the next four or five blocks with him crying and carrying on. I did a great job of keeping my cool until about the fourth step after he rejoined us. I was secretly cursing my wife for making this ridiculous request to walk 'safely' home. The rest of the walk was filled with, "Be quiet," and "Enough," and "Quit whining." All very successful … NOT! The other two children were no better, "I'm hungry," "I'm tired," and, "I don't want to walk home!" Every other step was filled with more whining, more complaining and more frustration on my part. Anyone who saw us or heard us had to think we were all nuts; myself included for trying to handle this on my own.

I thought that making it home would solve all the problems. Again, I was mistaken. We opened the garage and started to walk in the house. I calmly asked the five-year-old to go to his room and take a break. He walked in the house first, followed by his seven-year-old sister. He was so upset; I'm sure in his defense, he thought slamming the door as hard as he could, would somehow make it all better. Little did he know his older sister had grabbed onto the door frame to take off her shoes. The scream she let out was nothing short of amazing and probably heard by the teachers up at the school.

The next few moments are still a blur, but I'll do my best to recount the misery I was in. I remember checking for injury, sending the boy to his room, grabbing an ice pack, hearing, "I'm hungry" again and not much else.

As things calmed down we all sat at the kitchen table to eat a snack. I tried to reflect with them about what had occurred since leaving our house only an hour and a half earlier. Good God, it seemed like an eternity, not just 90 minutes. It was a great moment of reflection only to be interrupted by the doorbell. The neighbor girl had come to ask the kids to play. We had just finished our snack so I decided to let them go out to ride bikes, thinking maybe some time with friends would make this night better. I told the neighbor that we would come out through the garage.

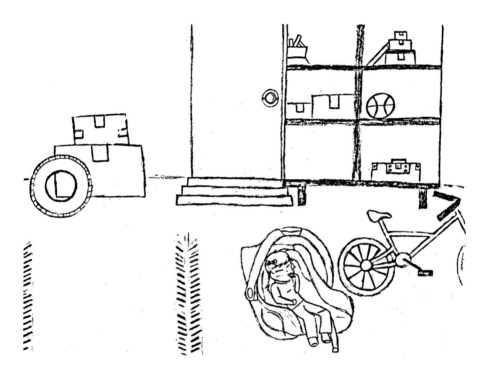

As I opened the door to the garage and looked out I had the worst feeling imaginable. All the other issues of the night seemed minute. There, in the middle of the garage, sat the baby carrier. It was right where I set it down when the screaming began a half hour earlier. In that baby carrier was my four-month-old, sound asleep. Who knows how long my darling would have been out there had my neighbor not come to play? It's Okay.

Forgotten

I was a full-time working mom and my husband and I were trying to successfully raise three boys. My 'work' job required that I offer time, effort and focus while I was on the job. Being good at my job wasn't enough and wasn't an option, I always strove to be exceptional. And to be honest, I am and always have been pretty darn good at my job. The problem lay in the fact that I expected even more out of myself when I was doing my 'mom' job. Unfortunately, something had to give. Burning both ends will somehow leave you with nothing in the middle.

The first time it happened, my excuse was pretty poor. As I rushed in to pick up my little guy from daycare an HOUR late … yes, an HOUR, the only excuse I had to offer was, "I read the clock wrong." Pathetically enough, it was true. I should probably leave out the fact that I am an elementary school teacher—reading the clock should be a given for me. The truth was I got busy working and preparing for the days to come. I kept glancing at the clock, but somehow was only looking at the minute hand, thinking it was the hour hand. I thought it was nearing the 5:30 pm hour, but really it was 6:30 pm. I was as apologetic as any mortified mother could be. The daycare provider was certainly pleasant but really not too happy. Who knows what she really thought. I mean, did she buy that a teacher misread the clock? It was the honest truth.

My second 'forgot my kid' story had less of an excuse than my first. You'd think since I took my 'mom' job so seriously, I'd have fewer of these stories to share! Anyway, I was at home one afternoon and was busy, busy and busier. Moms, you know what I mean. You are multitasking to no end; dinner, laundry, sorting mail, checking e-mail, writing thank you notes, filling out school paperwork, budgeting, and all the while carrying on a conversation with an old friend you haven't been able to touch base with for months.

Anyway, I was busy at home and this day of all days, I was supposed to pick up my fourth grade son from football. Granted, to give me some credit back, I was not the usual picker-upper (this somehow makes me feel a little better). A half-hour after I was supposed to be at practice, I realized my mistake. I don't think my car had ever seen the streets pass so quickly. I might add I am a bit of a rule follower, so speeding along was not easy for me, but I did it for my little guy. The little guy I FORGOT! I was frantic. My stomach was in knots. I hit every red light and there were cars lined up at every stop sign. Of course, this was pre-cell phone era, so I couldn't even call a friend, or the coach, or my hubby.

I arrived in the parking lot near where they had practiced. The sun had gone down and the night sky was overtaking the area. There he was, standing under a street light—probably the only light he could find. His helmet was in his hand and he was trying to look tough. I, of course, knew his looks and knew this 'tough' facade was really an 'I'm not going to cry' look. The coach had stuck around, but was obviously pretty perturbed with my tardiness and was sitting in his parked car. While I wasn't as worried about the coach—we all make mistakes—I couldn't get over how that boy of mine lost more and more courage as each minute passed while he was waiting for his mother. To this day, he can still make me feel bad about his 'forgotten' night many years ago. It's Okay.

Chopstick

After reading about the Target visit I had with my son a few chapters back (running over his hand with the cart … a hospital visit … stiches … etc.), you might think that I would have never tried to brave the store alone again. But, alas, as all good moms do, I thought surely something so terrible could never happen again! This amazing *mom of the year* story took place in a Kohl's department store.

My hubby was out of town on business and I was six months pregnant, shopping with my two children who were a respectable five and three. It was a busy Saturday morning, but I thought a shopping outing would be fun. NOT. You know how kids this age can be, running in and out of the racks while you're trying to shop; trying to check for sizes and seeing if the outfit is something they'll like and will *actually* wear.

My daughter came up to me so proud. "Look what I found!" It was a stick; kind of a cross between a pick-up-stick and a chopstick. My response lacked any sort of enthusiasm. "Great, have fun with that. Do you like the pink shirt or the yellow shirt better?" Okay, moving right along. I was done with the girls' section and we were on to the boys' section. I repeated the exhausting shopping-with-two-kids-process.

The kids were running in and out of the racks, one running clockwise, the other running counter-clockwise and then, BAM. The ear-piercing screaming began.

My three-year-old girl had that cross between a pick-up-stick and a chopstick shoved up her nose. There was blood everywhere (flash-backs to my Target story were vividly flooding my brain). Two employees passed right by me. There I was, six months pregnant, sitting on the floor, trying to contain the blood with something (anything!) in my purse. My purse was dumped out all over the floor of the boys' department. I think I found a dirty Kleenex or two. My daughter continued her screaming and crying and bleeding.

Then my son started in; crying and carrying on. "It's my entire fault. I ran into her." So you can imagine ... cries and blood from one, cries of shame from another and cries from the six-month pregnant mommy. I started yelling. "Can somebody please help me!?!??!" Finally, another mom shopper stopped and offered help in the form of baby wipes and tried to help me calm my kids down. I eventually got everyone settled and ushered them back to the car. I'm oversimplifying this process; just so we can move on with the story. It was absolutely awful.

Our doctor's house was in a nearby neighborhood, so I drove there, but no one was home. I tried his cell, but there was no answer. My aunt and uncle lived in the next neighborhood, so I took the kids there. I just needed some damn help. We finally got my little lady's nose to stop bleeding and got everyone calmed down (myself included). My aunt suggested putting Preparation-H in her nose. She said cheerfully, "It fixes everything!" I was somewhat distracted by the thought of the dad in *My Big Fat Greek Wedding* with his Windex fetish, thinking it would fix any ailment.

I kindly refused the Preparation-H that day, but couldn't stop the recurring images of my daughter's brain bleeding because she jammed a chopstick so far up her nose. As with all mothering stories, there are lessons to be learned.

Lesson 1: Chopsticks should stay at sushi restaurants.

Lesson 2: The fastest way to earning *mom of the year* is to NOT let your kids find and play with random trash toys that lie on the floors of department stores

It's Okay.

Restraints

We live by a small creek lined with trees which provided hours of entertainment for my boys when they were young. The boys were two years apart and often spent time at the creek with their friends climbing trees and building forts. Many new homes were being built in our neighborhood at the time, so there was an abundance of scrap wood lying around that was perfect for building projects. Hammers and nails were constantly being confiscated from my husband's workbench and the boys always seemed to have a project going. They'd disappear for hours in those trees down the street. There was climbing, laughing, building, and **even falling,** which brings to mind the following story.

My husband and I were in the front yard one crisp, fall day, when we spotted one of our boys limping up the hill; one filthy hand on his thigh. "Mom, Mom, where's the Band-Aids?" He repeated this several times, getting louder and louder as he spoke. Now, it's important for you to fully visualize the scene from our perspective. Our boy was about seven at the time, skinny as a rail, with bow legs the diameter of my wrist. When we asked to see his injury, our boy refused to move his hand; he also refused to let any tears escape from his huge, brown eyes. Finally, as my husband pried his hand away, we knew that a trip to the ER was in our future.

After frantically collecting our older son from the tree that he'd *not* bothered to climb out of (apparently not concerned for the gaping hole in his brother's thigh), we rushed the boys into the car and headed for the hospital. On the way, the story was reluctantly revealed by the boys. It seems that our injured son was up pretty high in the tree attempting to nail down a board when he slipped and fell. On the way down, his upper leg was impaled by a branch, which he'd yanked out before hobbling up the street. The gash was perfectly round and about the size of a dime.

After filling out mounds of paperwork at the ER, we were escorted back to an examination room. Upon assessment of the situation, the doctor determined that our son would need stitches. As he approached my boy with the needle, my angelic son started screaming bloody murder. "Touch me and I'll sue!" He shouted this embarrassing statement over and over and over. The incredulous physician was quite clearly taken aback and hesitated for a few minutes. He left the room and returned with what looked like a miniature straight jacket that he managed to wrap around the seven-year-old's writhing body. My son was still clearly in distress, but could do nothing about it, as his arms were now held firmly in place so that the splinters could be extracted and the stitches administered. Believe me, I would have been happy to have donned Harry Potter's invisibility cape at that point, as I was obviously *not* a model parent with a docile, compliant child.

Many years later, after the boys became responsible adults, the full story of that day came out. It seemed that the accident was a bit more involved than what they'd originally relayed and my son was lucky that a 'hole' in his leg was his only injury. Believe it or not, that same fierce determination and ability to speak his mind enabled that boy of mine to graduate from college with honors and to become a successful mechanical engineer. Yes, he's still building things. Maybe I wasn't such a bad mom after all! It's Okay.

Escapee

So my two-year-old went for a neighborhood visit—ON HIS OWN! Yes, you might think I was tending to several other children or that it was actually a babysitter watching my only son; well, neither is the case. My husband and I were enjoying some peace while our two-year-old was napping. I think we were downstairs looking for deals on the computer or playing a computer game. I don't suppose it really matters what WE were doing, but rather what my little boy was up to.

As I may have mentioned, my boy was upstairs napping. He was a great sleeper at the time, so we had zero concerns about being in the basement while he was sleeping. We came upstairs after a while to check on him, and **could not** find him! We started to panic after searching every square inch of the house and not locating him. As a last ditch effort, my husband went out the front door in search of our toddler. Terrible images were flashing through my mind. The worst image was being visited by a police officer who had dispersed my son to a family that would actually watch him. This may have been dramatic thinking, but your mind tends to wander when your little boy is missing.

After some frantic pacing in my living room for I don't know how long, my husband returned with my two-year-in tow. My pant-less son was returned, blanket and all, from up the street on the corner. He apparently had headed up the street to check in on a neighborhood construction zone. Earlier that day, my husband and my son had gone to look at a cement truck and Bobcat that were busy working on a neighbor's driveway. In our defense, the boy had always been (and still is) obsessed with construction vehicles. It must have been the only thing on his mind since he and his dad had made the morning visit to the corner construction zone.

That day, we learned a little lesson: quiet is not necessarily a good thing! We installed major door locks after that day and still continue to check them when the kids are out of our sight (yes, we've managed to raise more children than just that curious two-year-old!). It's Okay.

Electrocuted

My son always loved to 'tinker' with things. He was, and still is, a very hands-on kind of person. He was good at puzzles, *loved* Legos and played for hours creating work projects. I always let him play with things that weren't really toys. I'd let him rummage around the cabinets for bowls, spoons, etc. I suppose at this point I should put in a plug for my now husband, who was at the time, the man I was dating. He DID NOT approve of me letting my boy 'tinker' with things the way I did and assured me that he was going to end up hurt. He'd repeat, on a fairly regular basis, "Those things are not toys."

Anyway, I was allowing my son to 'play' in the kitchen one day while I was cooking and cleaning. He was two at the time and busy as ever. Soon, he had a knife from the silverware drawer (a butter knife that goes with the silverware set, not a paring knife; I'm not *that* dumb). Maybe he had gotten it out of the dishwasher, I'm not sure. He was going around the kitchen 'fixing' things, poking it in the cabinets, drawers, etc. I remember him asking if he could fix the dishwasher. I said something like, "Sure, you would be good at that," trying to encourage him.

The next thing I knew, he had stuck the knife up into the handle of this old-fashioned dishwasher. He flew backward, because the knife had touched the electrical wires and he had almost electrocuted himself! The knife was black where it had touched the wires. For goodness sakes, I could have taken out my own child just by letting him be curious and trying to encourage his talents.

Fortunately, he wasn't really hurt. It was especially difficult for me to share this story with the man I was dating at the time. While we can laugh about it today, it was anything but a laughing matter when it occurred.

I've always encouraged my son to use his talents; granted I became a little more in tune with which talents he was using (so that he would stay safe). He now works in Mechanical Design Technology. Maybe my 'encouraging' that day taught him a thing or two about his future career. Maybe I didn't screw up that bad after all! It's Okay.

CHAPTER IX

Most Mortifying Mommy Moment

T here's really no way around being embarrassed at least a million times during parenthood. Some moments are definitely more horrifying than others, but these moments or mishaps happen more often than parents care to admit. Whether you are in the store with a screaming toddler, have a poop explosion at the most inopportune time or just have a child being disrespectful, it happens. The title of this chapter only includes moms! This doesn't mean that dads don't get embarrassed; it just has been my experience that dads seem to have thicker skin than us we-have-to-keep-it-all-together moms do!

Times when you can laugh along with the embarrassment and play down how you are really feeling inside are for sure the best. But, sometimes the moments are so awfully great that you just have to escape the situation you are in as quickly as possible. It's moments like these that you pray the people around you don't know exactly what is happening or don't understand the extent to which your pride has plummeted.

I never understood why people don't tell you about how these moments will leave you feeling. Why, when you leave the hospital, is there not a manual entitled, *Some days everything that can go wrong, will?* It's almost like life with your new little being is supposed to be perfect and when it's not, you feel like a failure. Life with children creates one mess after another. Granted, there are just as many joyful moments as humiliating ones, but, still! A little preparation would be helpful.

So, here it is. The truth! Parenthood is one awkward, uncomfortable, excruciating moment after another. Just embrace it. Laugh at yourself. Put a smile on your face and keep on walking out that door. Know that things will go wrong when you least expect and when you least want them to. If we really let go of our judgments of others, maybe they, too, will not judge us in our moments of weakness and disgrace.

Branded and Scolded

What a beautiful morning it was. We even got out the door on time. Life couldn't have been better. The baby was in the wagon, the four-year-old was on her bike and the two school-age kids were walking without complaint. School day, here we come! As we embarked down the large hill just outside of our house, my school-age boy began crashing my morning glory; he started chasing his bike-riding, little sister. It was not good. It was not good at all and I had to put the kibosh on that activity quickly.

Thinking things could still be wonderful, we continued our stroll. Around the corner we went, across a small intersection, and only had two blocks left. Someone upstairs must have thought it was funny that I wanted to have a wonderful morning and decided to test me; to change things up a bit. My school-age son began chasing his little, bike-riding sister again. Only this time it was right near the busiest street in front of the school. At the end of the block stood the school-age crossing guards, the adult supervisor and, of course, a police officer to help maintain traffic.

My shouts were heard only by the officer and the supervisor. Apparently my children needed their ears checked that morning. I yelled for them to stop, to come back, that someone was going to get hurt! It was then that I got the disgusted look from the supervisor. You know the one that said, "What the hell is wrong with this mom? Letting her kids run wild near this busy street?" I'm sure she was just concerned (as I was, as well), that my four-year-old was going to lose control and drive her little training wheels right into the street in front of on-coming traffic. The supervisor and police officer shared some looks. I might add that I was practically *running* after my children then; they had gotten so far ahead of me.

I caught up to them, gave them a good scolding, and then proceeded to tell them how embarrassed I was that the supervisor and police officer saw the whole incident. As we approached the street, I tried to salvage my reputation. "So sorry, they apparently didn't hear me say to come back. I've talked with them about what happened and that it wasn't safe." The supervisor's response was somewhat caring. "I was just worried she was going to lose control." The police officer had nothing to say, but was eyeing me the whole time.

We got across the first street and had to wait on the corner to cross to the school. I had the wagon and there were probably 12 people waiting to cross the street. I couldn't get up on the sidewalk, so the wagon was sticking out in the street. Oh well, I thought. At least there were no cars that way, and I knew we would be crossing soon. I began small talk with the school-age crossing guards (trying to show the supervisor and police officer that I was a decent person). It was finally about time for us to cross. I started to take off, when I heard a crash behind me.

Well, when we started our day, it was going so wonderfully that I apparently didn't feel the need to buckle in my one-year-old. Oops. The supervisor and police officer witnessed me pull the wagon (not knowing my one-year-old was standing up behind me) only to have my baby fall out on her head. Dear Lord. Throw me a bone. I scooped her up as quickly as I could, made no more small talk and walked as fast as I could the rest of the way to the school with the baby on my hip.

The school kids got dropped off; of course, not before I let my son have it one more time. Like an adult temper tantrum before school was really going to sink in. At least I was quiet about it. I don't think anyone else heard my shenanigan. At the front of the school, I put the baby back in the wagon, double-checked the buckle and started heading back toward the police officer for more humiliation. It was then that I saw a mom dealing with a toddler who was throwing a fit about being in his stroller. She seemed equally as frustrated as I, but tried to smile as she passed the principal. Seriously, how do kids know when to throw fits?

I touched her arm and leaned in. "Hey, my baby just fell out of the wagon, **on her head**, in the middle of the street, *right in front of the police officer* because I hadn't buckled her in. That should make you feel better!" Her response was said with a wide smile. "Actually, it does. Thanks!" It's Okay.

Kid Leash

Right before I had my first child, a beautiful baby girl, I noticed a trend popping up that I swore to myself I would NEVER follow. Backpack Leashes! I noticed kids, usually toddlers or preschoolers, wearing backpacks designed to look like monkeys. I have to admit that the designer was very cleaver, trying not to make the backpacks look like actual leashes. They were very cute, with the arms and legs of the monkey serving as the straps—essentially locking the child to the bag. They weren't too big, had a little pocket to put things in and looked like they were giving the kids a hug. The part that was so vastly unappealing about these items, were that they also featured a lengthy tail with a loop at the end, for the parent, or whomever happened to be supervising the child, to hold. There was really no way around it … these people were walking around with their kid on a leash.

Backpack leashes popped up in the zoo, the mall, the GROCERY STORE (for heaven's sake, that's what they make carts with buckles for) and I promised myself that I would never need something like that to contain MY child. Fast forward five years. My first born girl was almost five and my second little guy was about to turn one. I was with my in-laws exchanging gifts for Christmas and an adoring cousin presented us with a gift containing a few different items. Among them—a monkey backpack! No, no, no! She was the mother of two boys; she laughed and said that I might find that this awful kid leash would come in handy with my son. Deep breaths! Sigh!

My good manners, thank heavens, did kick in. They kicked in just in time to choke back any derision and any idea I had to offer back this dog-like gift. Instead, a warm and convincing thank you came out. As this was all occurring, I was mentally re-vowing never to use the thing and to chuck it in the donation box as soon as I got home. Problem solved, right? Wrong! My daughter chimed in, "Oh Mom, I've wanted one of these forever!" Inwardly then, I groaned, but I had faith that she'd forget about it before it became an issue.

A few short months later, we had plans to meet some friends at the zoo. The monkey backpack had NOT made it into the donation box yet and was, instead, at the top of my little girl's toy box. My daughter gleefully pulled it out just as we were heading out the door to bring with us to the zoo. Okay, I can handle this. I thought it was no big deal. We would just leave it in the car. Oh no, it wasn't that easy. Once we got to the zoo, she insisted I help her get it on. My heart sank. I kept the tail unsnapped, tucked into the diaper bag, hoping she'd at least forget the most mortifying part.

My enthusiasm was dampened, but not gone completely. I kept thinking, "This will be all right." Then, she very excitedly reminded me, "Mom, put the monkey's tail on!" She was so pleasantly pleased with herself for remembering. As a last ditch effort, I attached the tail and handed her the end to hold. That way people would know it was all her idea, not mine! She carried it for a while, but soon tired of that. She ran back to me and said, "Here Mom, you have to hold it." I tried to convince her that she should continue to carry it (please, I pleaded with God), to which she responded, "No Mom, you need it so you can keep track of me."

That day, I walked through the zoo, with my nearly-five-year-old— on a leash. My pride trampled with every step I took. It's okay.

Dentist Don'ts

Oh, this is so embarrassing to admit. But, here it goes. We were horrible about brushing our kids' teeth and making them brush their own teeth. I know we should have done it twice a day, but we were content if we got it done once. This should have been a critical part of our morning, but we HATED fighting this battle more than any. Mornings were crazy enough as it was, getting ourselves and three children ready for the day, and to add the teeth brushing would have put us over the edge some days. Most nights their pearly whites got extra clean, but running out the door in the morning, we were lucky to be on time to work, let alone tend to the teeth of our children.

Now that our two oldest are more proficient at brushing, they help get the process going and finished with more success than before. It really is a shame that they understood the importance of this task. That is since they felt guilty enough about it to tattle on me to our dentist.

We were in for one of their check-ups and the dentist was discussing with my children how often to brush and the techniques of brushing. My then four-year-old just had to chime in. "MOM ... we've only been brushing at night. I told you we should brush more." I tried to avoid eye contact with the dentist. His face would say it all. The look he would give me would only add to the shame and humiliation I felt. Oh, again, how embarrassing. It's Okay.

Returned

I suppose I should just be thankful that my children were not run over by a car, but having your children brought to you AT WORK after being found by a local police officer is MORTIFYING! It's a good thing that we lived in a community where everyone knew everyone and that this particular police officer had a relationship with my husband. You see, my husband owned the local donut shop and I hate to be stereotypical, but most of the police officers were on a first name basis with the hubby. In this instance, it sure came in handy.

My children were supposed to be napping and the babysitter was being paid to keep my children safe and *at home*. Neither of these things happened that day and I ended up looking like the irresponsible mother. My kids were around the ages of three and one at the time. Both had a mind of their own and seemed to have the 'street smarts' of children far older than the both of them. I don't know exactly where they thought they were going that day, but their adventure turned out to be an exciting one.

After crossing a four-lane road and two other two-way streets, they were thankfully spotted by the police officer. They were nearly approaching one of the busiest intersections when the officer must have sensed something was amiss. I mean, who wouldn't wonder about a three-year-old dragging a one-year-old in his diaper ALL ALONE? It didn't take the officer long to figure out who these precious little people belonged to.

He immediately put them in the police car and drove them to the donut shop. I wish that I could have seen my husband's face when the officer walked in with his two youngest children in hand. I would have been happy if he would have just handled the situation, taken them home and let the babysitter have it. But, alas, my husband's temper would have gotten the better of him and he knew that I was more suited for the job.

There I was, busy at work, not expecting my husband to toddle in with my two youngest kids. He didn't mean to create a scene, but how could he not? My boy didn't even have pants on. While he tried to quietly tell me about the events that had transpired, the three-year-old shouted out about her ride in the police car and how cool it was that they got picked up off the street. It seemed that everyone I worked with was standing outside of their offices, just staring at me.

Again, I should have been thankful that my children did not get hurt. I should have been grateful to the police officer for not arresting us or taking our children away for being unsuitable parents. I should have been pleased that my husband didn't lose his cool. I should have been appreciative that the situation wasn't worse than it was. BUT, all I could feel was embarrassment and shame right down to the core. It's Okay.

Office Obstacles

I've always thought that a great idea for a reality TV show would be to video tape moms and their children while they wait for the doctor inside a pediatrician's exam room. I really felt like it was cruel and unusual punishment to put me and my three small children (all under the age of five at the time), in a 10x10 room with nothing in it except a small round spinning chair and a table with crinkly white paper on it. Oh, and I'm forgetting the hand sanitizer wall unit that was within reach for two of my children.

As a mom, you sit there and ask the children to be on their best behavior. You feel like everyone on the outside of the exam room is listening to you and judging not only your children's behavior, but also your parenting skills.

Our name was finally called to head back to the exam room and the mortifying morning in question went like this.

At first my children did wonderfully. They sat and read the gently used children's books that were in the bucket on the floor. But, as curiosity grew and boredom set in, they ventured over to the spinning doctor's chair and began to push each other around. The laughing, giggling and shrieks of joy began. They were having so much fun, but I could sense what was coming.

After a few minutes, they began to fight over the chair. Next thing I knew, one of my children had run over the other child's finger. Then all hell broke loose. I finally got them calmed down and glanced at my watch. Are you kidding? It felt like an eternity had passed, but in reality, it had only been five minutes.

As time ticked on, my children found interest in the examination table. At first the crinkly paper was enough to satisfy them, but they soon tired of that and began to jump and push one another off the table. At this point, I was so exhausted from trying to keep them under control that I just gave in and let them jump. I gave up the battle, secretly hoping that the pediatrician visit I was having wouldn't turn into an ER visit.

The volume in the room escalated and I tried to regain control, but it was too late. They were having too much fun. My thoughts were streaming. Should I threaten to spank them? Was there a staff member outside the door that would hear my threat? Should I put them in time out? Would that same staff member laugh at me for trying to force a time out in this hell box we were stuck in? Should I break out the cell phone? Or the iPad? Wouldn't I be an even worse mother when they heard I had caved?

While I was trying to decide my next course of action, the door finally opened and in walked the doctor, just as one of my children plummeted from the exam table. My other child then crashed into the wall with the doctor chair and to top it all off, the baby puked all over me.

I cleaned myself off, gathered up my children and got everyone (including myself) under control as the doctor began the examination.

The kids were being so good and suddenly I felt a sense of pride. Maybe this was going to be alright! If we could just make it a few more minutes; I was praying for the best. Forget about those three questions I had, I could no longer even remember what they were. If they were truly pressing, I'd call the nurse later when I actually had a moment to think.

As the doctor neared the end of his examination, my three-year-old stated that she had to go to the bathroom. The doctor told me it was okay to take her, he didn't want an accident. Yeah, okay, great. My thoughts streamed again. I would take her to the bathroom with these other two, just in time for you to go see another patient and then I'd be locked in this 10x10 box for another twenty minutes. I think not. I asked that we just quickly try to finish the exam and then I'd run her. I assumed that she could hold it for another few minutes. The doctor hesitated, repeated that it was okay for me to take her, explained again that he would wait for us and that he didn't want an accident.

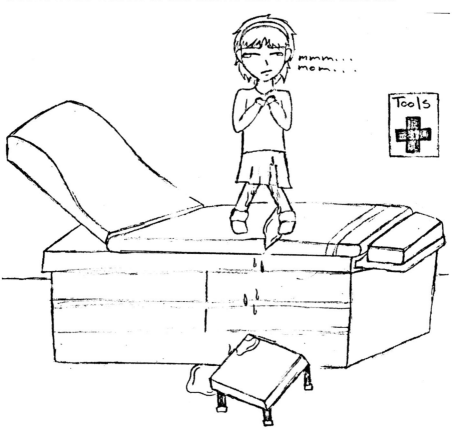

Seriously, he was wasting time. I reassured him that it would be okay and if we could please just continue. He concluded the exam and began to say goodbye to me and the children. I was tickled! We did it! My new thoughts were to run to the bathroom.

Oh no, too late. Before he walked out the door, he turned to the unmistakable sound of urine cascading from the top of the exam table. Just then, my three-year-old took a seat on the table, amidst her pool of urine, with relief washed all over her face. Her entire bladder had been emptied on the table and created a magnificent waterfall from the table to the floor. At that moment, humiliation got the better of me! It's Okay.

Drowned Rats

So, imagine a three-week, post-partum mother trying to take her four children swimming. Of course, I was not planning to reveal my un-tanned, over-weight, still-looking-pregnant body in a swimsuit. I had on a ridiculous black nursing tank and long black shorts (trying to cover every ounce of my body I could with black, hoping to slim down the parts that were actually covered). While this did not help my 'just-had-a-baby' look, you can't blame me for trying.

It was spring and our children had not been swimming since the previous summer. Our older two were pretty good swimmers and our third child was in floats. Perfect! Wouldn't have to get in! If necessary, my husband was going to take one for the team, but he was doing everything possible to avoid the water as well.

It was our first time at our friends' pool and things were a little jumbled as we arrived. My husband had gone back to the car a few times for things we forgot and the kids were really anxious to get in the pool. This was right at the moment that the newborn chose to cry and so I was tending to her as well. "Fine, go swim," I said this reluctantly knowing my husband was not back yet. All was fine, EXCEPT, we didn't go over the pool parameters, like we usually did.

So, they were all swimming. My eyes went back and forth from baby to kids to baby to kids to baby to kids. It was then that my husband arrived back at the gate. He needed to be let in. I averted my eyes only long enough to see that he was being let in by someone else at the pool. As I turned back around, I noticed my flailing son. No! No, no, no! Quickly, I set the baby down and ran to the other side of the pool to grab my flailing son.

He was just out of reach of my hand. NO! I didn't even have a suit on. Ugh, if only I could have avoided that dreaded moment. I jumped in, fully clothed, fully post-partum and grabbed my son. Seriously, I should have been worried about my kid, but he was fine. He didn't even go under—just flailed (apparently a little gun shy about using the strokes he had learned the previous summer). He panicked and I was drenched. I dragged my flabby body over to the ladder and tried to think about my next steps. I had no change of clothes, we had just got there and already I was feeling defeated and ready to go home.

Well, I lost parent of the year for having a nearly-drowned son, but I think it had to be worth something that I sucked it up and stayed for the next three hours in soaking wet clothes! Not only had everyone at the pool witnessed the whole scene, but they watched closely as I dragged my flabby self out and used one of my children's towels to dry off the best I could. It's Okay.

Bottle Pop

One afternoon we headed over to a friend's house with our two children for a party. While we were so excited to go, I was a little anxious. At the time, we were the only couple that had children. Everyone enjoyed our children and loved to play with them, but have you ever taken two small children to a house that does not have any other children? Not to mention that these friends were all top notch professionals (making me feel even more nervous). It is not fun.

I knew I would not get to sit back and relax, just visiting with the friends I hadn't seen in months. I wasn't going to get to enjoy that glass of wine like I did before I had children. Instead I would be running around and making sure my kids did not break anything or fall into the pool, and I'd be doing all this while being watched like a hawk by my childless friends feeling judged with every move I made.

After several hours of chasing my kids around, I just wanted to sit and enjoy my friends' company for a few minutes. I had brought a bottle for my two-year-old. Yes, she was still on the bottle. I poured some milk into the bottle, expecting her to sit back and relax for a few moments, allowing me to converse with the adults for a brief time. Instead, she began to throw a fit. This was not a whiney fit that signaled she wasn't getting what she wanted. It was a full blown, arms and legs flailing, fit. I couldn't figure out why she was so upset, but then I noticed a can of Coke on the table. She wanted a drink of the pop.

At that moment, it was do or die for my long-deserved moment of peace where I could have an adult conversation. I did the unspeakable. I gave in to the temptation, emptied the milk out of the bottle and filled the bottle up with pop. I didn't care what anybody thought about me giving my two-year-old six ounces of Coca-Cola. I just wanted to relax for a few minutes. Might I add that it felt great! I got my moment, my well-deserved moment. I was on top of the world; that is, until I glanced across the table. There sat one of our dear college friends who happened to be a pediatrician. Yes, a doctor who would die if one of his patients was given pop in a bottle at the age of two. I wanted to crumble, but that wine and conversation were too darn amazing! Oh well, moment had and moment enjoyed. It's Okay.

Store Misery

My most embarrassing moment happened at the grocery store when my kids were about four and five years old. Let me explain that I had five-year-old twins, both girls, and a four-year-old son. Times were difficult for many years, but at that point in my parenting, making a trip to the store was something that I did not worry about or dread like I had in the past. Well, I didn't think I had to worry, but like with all parenting moments, things fall apart when you least expect them to.

It was right before Christmas and I was going to be hosting a dinner party for about 12 members of our extended family. I was planning to pick up a couple bottles of wine for the occasion. Now you might need a little background here. We *did not* drink alcohol at the time. With our three children now all being pre-teens, that's a different story; a well-deserved glass of wine is needed occasionally. But, at the time, we didn't even keep an ounce of alcohol in the house. We had always told our kids that alcohol was 'yucky' and it would make them sick.

Looking back, these words may not have been the best way to talk to our children about alcohol, but as with most things, hindsight is always 20/20.

Let's fast forward to the grocery store. I had a heaping cart full of groceries and kids in tow. Last stop was the liquor aisle. I scanned the wine selection and quickly grabbed a bottle in each hand and started to put them in the cart. That was when the humiliation began. Oh, and did I mention yet that there was an off-duty officer standing guard? Where was he standing guard you might ask? He was nowhere other than right next to the wine section. No big deal, right? I was old enough to buy alcohol. Wrong! The second I placed the bottles in the cart my kids ERUPTED into protest mode. I swear they were almost in tears while they shouting out. "Mommy, why are you buying alcohol? Please don't buy alcohol." And the topper, "You know it makes you sick! Don't drink it mommy."

I was mortified as I immediately returned the bottles to the shelf, put my head down and headed for the nearest checkout line. Needless to say it was an alcohol-free holiday dinner. I can only imagine what people around me were thinking and the look on the officer's face was unforgettable. I was so embarrassed!!! It's Okay.

Bright Red

Many parents remember taking their little ones to the pediatrician for their immunizations. It's particularly difficult when you're a new parent and your child is still an infant. By the time your child is ready to start kindergarten, parents usually feel a bit more comfortable with trips to the doctor's office. That's the way I felt on the day that I took my oldest son to his pediatrician's office for his kindergarten physical. Since I was a teacher and the doctor was a member of the school board, our paths had crossed on several different occasions. I felt fairly comfortable with the man; yet, clearly, from my story below … my child did NOT!

After the usual physical examination, the doctor announced that my son would be getting some immunizations that day. Of course, my son hadn't a clue about what that word meant. Not until he saw the needle, that is! As soon as he realized that he was getting the dreaded 'shot,' he ran out of the exam room screaming at the top of his lungs! He shot out of that room faster than I could grab him, jettisoned to the waiting room, crawled under a chair and continued to scream like a wild animal.

Now, if you'll remember, the doctor was an esteemed member of the school board and I was one of the district's teachers. I'd never felt so humiliated and was sure that the doctor was wondering how I could possibly be an effective teacher if I couldn't even control my own child. I wanted to crawl under that chair myself; I was so embarrassed. Somehow the nurses and I managed to get my son back into the examination room and he received those shots. However, I felt like my reputation had taken more of a blow that day than my son's little arm! It's Okay.

Library Loser

All the parenting books talk about how important it is to provide literacy opportunities for your child from a young age. Libraries even try to accommodate by offering child programs, story times and even encouraging children to come to the 'children's section' of the library. But, really, libraries aren't actually kid friendly. Most of the time librarians don't even seem to want kids around. I mean, kids move books, knock them off the shelves and more than anything, they are louder than freight trains in these quiet sanctuaries.

I tried to make library time consistent so that my children would understand how to use the library appropriately. We made it a rule that we would check out movies at the end, after picking books or attending programs, so that it would be an incentive for them to behave. If they didn't behave, there would be no movies. I had even had to, on occasion, drop movies in the outside drop box on the way out, because something happened at check-out or walking out the door. I really had tried.

Well, one day was particularly rough. I had to fill out some paperwork at the front desk while checking out. The baby was strapped in the stroller, though not happily, and the other three were supposed to be standing by me. The trouble began. There was running, tickling, tripping, grabbing, squealing ... endless shameful behavior. I made them all sit against the desk in front of me and threatened to take away the movies. Two of them obliged, but the third continued to make a scene. She was running ALL OVER and being REALLY loud. Then, the baby began to cry. Sweat was coming out of every orifice of my body and I just needed to get out of that awful, quiet place.

I finally got the paperwork done, though not without one hand always grabbing or swatting at a kid. My face had a permanent nasty glare glued to it. I had to look ridiculous. The line behind me was getting longer and my control was diminishing by the second. I had the irritated young woman who was checking me out put back my naughtiest child's movie and thought *that* might do the trick. NOPE. Things only got worse. I scooped up my things and headed for the door. If they didn't follow, I was sure some nice stranger would have given them a lift home. I just kept walking. At that point, I didn't care if they all didn't make it to the car. I might also add that at that moment, the baby was no longer just crying, but screaming for dear life and wriggling her body every which way to try to dislodge herself from the straps that were holding her into the stroller.

The bag was ridiculously full. I pushed the stroller with one hand and tried to hold the bag and my purse in the other. There was no time to put anything in the basket. I had to get out ... RIGHT then. I saw two children following out of the corner of my eye, phew, they were coming. They knew I meant business. But, where was that third one? I wasn't going to look back. At that moment, something happened to my body. I was propelled forward by what felt like a karate kick to my lower back. I stayed strong and still didn't turn around, but realized that my four-year-old had pushed me with all of her might. She was darn strong.

We were almost to the door. The baby was still screaming, two of my children were scrambling to keep up with their enraged mother and one insane child was, I thought, just trailing behind. And then it happened again. Karate kick #2, and even stronger than the first. There was a short break, and then there it was again. I realized that my four-year-old was stopping, waiting for me to get a little ahead and then running at full speed to push me as hard as she could. She continued this process four or five times until we hit the door to leave the library. Dear God, was she going to stop? My hands were full and I didn't have one free limb to grab her or scold her or scoop her up to carry her to the car.

I thought once we got to the door it would stop. We were parked a good block away and there was no way this could continue. Wrong. All the way to the car I was completely defenseless. There'd be a major push, then short relief, only for the time it took her to wait to get at a sprinting pace to ram into me again. My rage continued to build; my pride dwindled by the nanoseconds. I was silently willing this punishment on me by my four-year-old to stop. The parking lot was FULL of respectable patrons awaiting their quiet time in the library. The only blessing for them was that we were no longer inside!

My karate chopping four-year-old served time in her room for hours once we actually got home. My pride was somewhat regained once Dad got home to give me a much needed break. And, needless to say, after that visit we skipped library time for weeks. It's Okay.

CHAPTER X

Parent Confessionals ... You're Absolved

We all have them—those moments in parenting that we are least proud of. Those moments that we wish we could somehow take back. Those moments we pray our children won't remember. Those moments we never talk about. Oh, those moments. They are the ones we have a hard time getting 'real' about and they unfortunately happen to every human parent. It's in those moments that we sometimes put ourselves in time-out and imagine that we may never figure out this hell people call parenting.

Maybe you are a screamer. Maybe you spank your kids. Maybe you are a parent who needs two beers before bed or a smoke on the stoop once your kids are sound asleep. There is not a perfect parent out there. We all have issues; it's just that our issues are different than everyone else's issues, and some hide their issues better than others. Who wants to admit to failure? Who wants to admit help is needed?

It's really okay that we mess up. The important part is that we learn from our mess-ups, parent a little better the next time and teach our children that we can ALL learn from our mistakes.

This chapter is full of 'real' stories from parents; real stories that could not have been easy to share. It is definitely not tranquil to go public with thoughts, feelings and actions that we are not proud of. Kudos to them! These parents deserve a pat on the back for getting 'real' about mistakes they have made. We all know that when the moment hits, we are going to feel better knowing that we are not the only ones who need to confess.

Muffin Mom

Being a working mom with two kids definitely had its challenges. I felt the pains of guilt daily that I was not there for the little things in my boys' lives; that they spent too much time in daycare. I would lie to myself that I worked in order to give my family more, which often led to overindulging my boys with material things to feel better about it all. In reality, I liked to work. I needed work. I thrived on the social relationships that I got and continue to get from the work place. Work seems to have always been my sanity check as a mother. When I did stay home with our newborn children, I found my only sanity came from TV. My husband would get a kick out of hearing about my BFF's, Dr. Phil and Opera. Martha Stewart and Rachel Ray were my acquaintances that shared their dearest recipes and 'how to' guides for home improvement projects.

Looking back, however, things were really going quite well for my family of four. We had a great routine and had a pretty good sync established. Balance was key and my hubby and I worked to achieve that. The scales all tipped, well, rather, the scales went off the charts, when kindergarten hit for my oldest. For some reason, school made everything more difficult. It threw us a new curve ball that we were apparently not ready for.

A turning point in my parenting journey occurred when our son brought home a note asking for treats for the first holiday party in the classroom. My mom was always the room parent for my class as a child and she had set the bar high with her cookies and cupcakes. I greatly looked forward to each passing holiday when I was a kid, knowing that she would come through for me and my class. Wanting to continue the tradition and standard set by my mom, I excitedly signed up to bring treats for the party. I was going to continue the tradition. I dreamed of the perfect snack that would delight the youngsters. I had my heart set on wowing the pants off my son's classmates, and secretly wanted to impress the pants off his teacher!

Well, as the time ticked closer to the big event, my to-do list grew longer and longer and my work schedule became hectic. I needed to secure two Halloween costumes, candy for the trick-or-treaters, send cards to nieces and nephews and meet deadlines at work. I stressed about how I was going to get it all done with the time remaining and still make my 'to-die-for' treats.

I carefully weighed my options and went with store-bought cookies in the respective holiday colors. This was going to work, it had to work. I was stretched thin as it was. That was all I could handle. The tradition could start at the next holiday. My son had his costume, looked adorable, and we had cookies for the class. I walked confidently into the class like I had conquered the working mom battle. As I watched all the little ones arrive with their goodies, my heart began to sink. I watched trays of beautifully decorated homemade goodies brought wrapped in themed goodie bags. With each passing child, I felt my stomach turn over and over. By the time I had left the party, my store bought cookies were not touched and were pale in comparison to the pumpkin shaped muffins decorated with licorice smiles and M&M eyes.

I was devastated. I ruined my mother's amazing tradition, I let down my son and I felt as though I had failed as a parent. I cried to my secretary later, explaining to her my feelings of defeat and failure. She grabbed me boldly and snapped me back to reality. Her words were so stern, but looking back, so real. I try desperately to remember her carefully chosen words every time being a working mom is stressing me to the breaking point. "You will NEVER be *The Muffin Mom*!" She stressed that I didn't have to be *The Muffin Mom* in order to be a great parent. She then took time to remind me of all the things I already did daily that made me a wonderful mom.

At that moment, in my greatest defeat, I had to come to terms with the fact that I was not and will never be, *The Muffin Mom!* While I can cross that off the list of things I wanted to be as a mother, I will continue to be there for my kids in other ways that are equally important. There is still a part of me that secretly wishes I could be the working muffin mom, be there for my kids in gold medal style, but hey, it's just not in the hand of cards that's been dealt for me. It's Okay.

Listen Up

Our boy was anything but an angel. My wife and I both worked and we needed child care during the day. While I am sure that my little hellion was fed, diapered and kept within the daycare walls, I now think that he may have been smarter than I cared to believe at the time. The daycare our children went to sang songs, read books, promoted the ABC's and went on field trips. We paid a hefty amount to give our children a pleasant experience during the day while we worked to make a living.

My son, who as I may have mentioned was a tad ornery, started protesting that he did not want to go to daycare. While I was not the perfect parent, I believed at the time that I was pretty darn close. I figured that my son was no better during the day than he was at home and the reason he didn't want to go to daycare was because he tended to get into trouble. This was a well-respected daycare and I didn't have any reason to believe there was good cause not to send my darling back to this place day after day.

As with many things in life, parenting is often a do-the-best-you-can-at-the-time type job. Looking back there is always room for improvement and hindsight is typically 20/20. The reasons my son shared for not wanting to go to daycare threw up some pink flags for us, but they were never red enough to uproot our children and try to find a new place. I now believe, many years later (and many untold stories told later in life by my older children), that my child was not treated fairly at daycare and was possibly abused in ways that could have shut the place down.

Among many issues, the worst of what my son endured, had to do with food. He still has food aversions as an adult and I hope to someday have the courage to apologize to him for not being more attentive. He really was naughty, but he was also wise beyond his years. While he had a comment for everything and an answer for every wrong deed, he was right about this one thing ... and I should have listened.

Be observant of your children. Be willing to listen to them. They are smart cookies and I know I learned far more from my children than they learned from me throughout my years of parenting. I suppose it's safe to say that they did a great job of raising me and I sure wasn't an easy sell! It's Okay.

SAHM! Really?

When my daughter was nine months old, I became a stay-at-home mom. I had been enjoying being back to work as a teacher, but finding out we had to move for my husband's career made me decide to try staying home for a year. Being at home meant connecting with other stay-at-home moms (or SAHMs as I sarcastically referred to us). I had play dates with other moms and their babies and I tried to connect online as well, using sites like Pinterest to get ideas. Almost immediately, I felt like I was in the middle of a gigantic competition to follow the latest philosophies, create the most educational activities and be the perfect parent that I didn't even know existed. Are you kidding me?

In my search to be a menial SAHM, I felt defeated. My kid kept me so busy that my only personal goal for each day was to shower. When was I going to create a sensory box filled with BPA free, organic, all natural, educational toys? How would I find time to build a paper holder/ easel to mount on the wall? I also became acutely aware that I was singlehandedly destroying the environment by being the only SAHM to not use cloth diapers. Gasp!

After a particularly overwhelming visit to an online message board, where the discussion centered on homemade baby foods and 'Elimination Communication,' I looked around my messy house feeling defeated. First off, I had yet to find information about how jar baby food damaged a child in any way. And, 'Elimination Communication' ... what is this? I had to look it up, which made me feel even more inadequate.

One day, I was determined to step up my game and decided to make a list of activity ideas while my daughter climbed all over me. Three minutes and a blank piece of paper later, I gave up. In a last ditch effort to keep her entertained I got out a cheap baby pool and blew it up in the family room. I threw in a bunch of her inferior toys and we had a blast playing together for the next nine minutes or so.

I may use the wrong diapers and often have the TV on in the background, which is sure to give my daughter ADHD, but in those awesome nine minutes I was reminded that I don't have to be the perfect SAHM. All that my little girl really needs is my imperfect self and the crazy amount of love I have for her. It's Okay.

Jail and Drugs

My husband and I have three grown boys. I had a boy prior to our marriage, he had a boy prior to our marriage and we had boy number three together. Our family is the proverbial yours, mine and ours! As we look back over the years, there are many stories that created worry, concern, guilt and anger. But, there are even more that were splattered full of joy.

When your kids are born, you want them to pursue whatever they are interested in, and whatever they are good at. At the same time, you have expectations. These expectations range from small day-to-day happenings that form the values you expect they will have one day, to the big future happenings like going to college. One expectation we always had for the boys was that they would *always* try their best at everything they did. Through the years, though, our other expectations changed. We adjusted to our children's personalities, needs and strengths, as well as their limitations (we all have weaknesses!).

So now, after all these years and having three grown sons, we've resorted to being proud of the fact that, "They're not on drugs and they're not in jail." That's our new standard! Let's just say the expectations lowered dramatically. In our years of growing as parents, we had friends who struggled through both these issues. We are still trying to figure out what it was, or still is, that kept our kids off drugs and out of jail. We are certainly proud that they have avoided both, but know that parenting is a 'do the best you can that day' type of thing.

There are thousands of stories to tell and countless lessons, for us and for the kids, which we have learned along the way. But, in the end, did we love them every day? Yes, absolutely. Did we try to do what was right, given the circumstances? Of course; well, at least most of the time. Did we attempt to teach them how to be responsible, caring people? Yes, and often more by example than by actually using words. Did they sometimes choose not to be responsible, caring people? Yes, probably too many times to count. When they made bad choices, did we attempt to give them an appropriate consequence? Yes, although some of them didn't really work in the short run, but I think the cumulative effect is more important.

So our standards changed over the years. Yours may, too! We are proud of our boys, proud of ourselves and know that we did the best darn job we could. What more could anyone ask for? It's Okay.

Hair Pull

"No one's gonna pull my baby's hair!" Oh, how I wish my husband would have been talking about his actual baby. But, sadly, he was referring to me, his dearly beloved wife. What can I say, we have a wonderful marriage and apparently, my husband still feels the need to protect me in a back alley brawl. Unfortunately, we never imagined that our home would become a war zone and that the alley brawl would occur daily in our living room.

Being the parents of four children has those unspeakably mesmerizing moments. You know, those ones where you stand and stare in awe of the little people you have created. Well, it also has those jaw-breaking, finger-nails-on-the-chalkboard, plane-crashing moments. It's in these moments that we've done things we never dreamed of doing.

We really have pretty good communication on the home front. My husband and I still enjoy one another's company. We like to catch up after a day of work and we often talk long after the children are in bed. When the below incident occurred, we were both overloaded at our jobs and our children were having more terrorizing moments than tantalizing ones.

We had about had it with our children misbehaving. We had had it with our screaming (which obviously was not working) and we decided we needed a change. One night after our children had gone to bed, we spent nearly two minutes designing a new plan. This was during the commercial break of a favorite show of ours, but the conversation was meaningful enough; at least to me, and we had high hopes for a great tomorrow.

Our new plan was in place. No screaming. Only calmly reminding the children one time and then following with a time-out if they did not comply. This time-out was to occur in their bedrooms, no exceptions. If they refused to go to their bedroom on their own, we would calmly escort them there. Great! It wouldn't take long before we were able to put our plan to good use.

The following day, we got home from a busy day at work. We managed to make it through the door with the thousands of items that accumulate during the day and got dinner started. Our third child tested our new plan. She punched her brother after he took a toy without asking. Calmly, I redirected her. She then kicked her brother. Oops, room time. I reminded her calmly that she could walk to her room or I could help her. She then tackled her brother and ignored my calm request.

I scooped her up and proceeded to her bedroom. She obviously did not like the new plan because she brutally assaulted me before we even made it to the stairway. I repositioned her so that the attack wouldn't hurt as badly. Somehow she got a limb free and grabbed my hair with all her might. I was working to reposition her one more time, when out of the blue came SUPER DAD—not really. He was not calm like we had discussed. Maybe he had forgotten our meaningful two-minute conversation we had had the previous night about our new plan.

Before I knew it, he had my daughter's hair firmly gripped in both his hands. He was not yanking it out of her head, but letting her know that hair pulling is not a fair way to fight. The attack was then over. There was no more flailing or hitting or hair-pulling from our daughter. Have I mentioned, yet, that she was only three at the time? However, we are talking about a *very* spirited three-year-old!

I sighed, the most disappointing sigh, and gave the most defeated look. "What about the new plan?" To which he calmly responded, "Ain't no one gonna pull my baby's hair!" Seriously? He is such a smart aleck.

That hurts!

After depositing my daughter in her room for her time-out, all I could do was laugh. While this may not have been a laughing matter, my out-of-control daughter *got it*. She was snapped back into reality and felt first-hand how the hair pulling felt. I do not condone my husband's behavior, but this was one of those back-alley times in our life that the brawl got a little out of hand. It's safe to say my husband has my back! It's Okay.

Bonding Blunder

It's okay not to instantly bond with your adoptive child. It's okay, right? I've come to the conclusion that bonding is a lifelong process, not an event. I'd venture to say that all parent/child relationships are a reflection of a lifelong bonding process. But, I'll go out on a limb and say that many adoptive parents have a tougher time with the process than those who give birth to their flesh and blood.

Unlike pregnancy, an adoption journey, particularly one that is international, can take many months, if not years. During the initial phase of the journey, you are busy compiling a dossier that includes FBI background checks, home studies, financial statements, photos, medical forms and emotional dissertations explaining to an adoption agency why you want to adopt and why you would make a fantastic parent.

A social worker examines your home and asks you a million questions ranging from your discipline philosophy to where the baby is going to sleep. Someone at the adoption agency has triple checked your dossier to make sure it is perfect before it is sent to bureaucrats in a country far, far away. You're sure those bureaucrats have no idea how much you want a baby. So, you worry. Did I say the right things? Do our pictures look good enough? Then, like a pregnancy, the waiting begins.

If you are lucky, as in our case, you only wait 13-14 months. Others are not as lucky, sometimes waiting up to five years for the adoption agency to call with the good news. During this time you are dreaming about your child. Is it a boy or a girl? Is the baby healthy? You wonder what the baby's personality will be like. That's all normal stuff to think about, isn't it? In the case of international adoption, you also think about things like, how old is my child? Is my child in an orphanage? If so, has someone taken an interest in my baby and held my baby? Does my baby have enough to eat every day? Has anyone talked to my baby? Has anyone held my baby in the middle of the night when she was awakened from a bad dream? You think about fetal alcohol syndrome, AIDS, Hepatitis, mental health impairments and maternal drug use. You wonder if you will ever know your baby's family medical history. Chances are you won't know any of this if you adopt from a foreign country.

Finally you receive the phone call you have been waiting for, for months. "We have a match for you," says the person on the phone from the adoption agency. This moment is probably like when you find out you are pregnant. The moment in time is indelibly etched in your mind. You will never forget it.

Just when you think the journey is over, you wait. You wait for permission to travel to your child's country. It drives you absolutely mad. Then, you endure a very, very long airplane ride to find yourself in a foreign land suffering from jet lag and scared out of your mind. You arrive at a hotel and wait. You wait for your baby to be placed in your arms. The wait is agonizing. Then the moment arrives.

The baby is handed over to you and she screams bloody murder when she sees your face, hears your voice and smells your smells. You might as well be an alien from outer space possessing three heads and 15 arms. Wait a minute. Where is that bonding moment? The one when the baby is placed on your chest and instantly settles down? In many cases of international adoption, it doesn't happen. This little person placed in your arms has her own little personality unshaped by your nature and your nurturing; she knows how she likes to be held and comforted, she knows the bedtime routine, she knows all her needs and you don't know any of them and she can't even tell you.

In many cases adoptive parents don't receive any information from the orphanage or foster family about the child. Talk about flying by the seat of your pants. So there you are on the other side of the world wondering how to comfort this baby who is, quite frankly, a stranger. Whether they will admit it or not, I believe many adoptive parents are terrified when they don't feel that instant bond with their child. I wish someone would tell them that it is okay to have to those thoughts.

I wish someone had told me that back in 1995. We adopted a baby who had a very difficult time attaching to us. She was the kind of adoptive baby the social worker warned us about. She cried every waking moment for about two months. It was miserable. A friend unknowingly hurt me to the core one day. I was in tears telling her about our baby's incessant crying and sleepless nights. Her response was, "You know you asked for this when you decided to adopt." I wonder if she would have said that to me if this was my birth child.

It's okay not to feel that instant Gerber baby bonding moment with your adoptive child. It's okay to ask yourself, "What did we get ourselves into?" It's okay to wish for different circumstances. They will eventually be different and they will be for the better. It just takes time. It's Okay.

Intolerable Infant

After a miscarriage and thinking I was *never* going to be pregnant, the second line finally appeared on my pregnancy test. I started planning and thinking about the kind of mom I was going to be. Of course, I was going to do it better than everybody else I knew. We decided not to find out what we were having so we could be surprised. Surprised we were when my water broke six weeks early. Because the baby was so early, we knew the possibility of NICU time was more than likely. A nurse from the NICU came to talk to us about what to expect. She had told us some of the concerns with a child being born this early. She also told us that little boys usually had more breathing and lung issues than girls. Immediately the guilt set in because I hadn't found out what I was having; I started to think that the hospital staff would have been better prepared if they had known whether the baby was a boy or girl.

Once my baby boy arrived, the nurses immediately took him down to the NICU to get him set up and to determine how he was doing. Everybody was so surprised at how well he was holding up. He didn't even require oxygen. When I finally was able to see him (several hours later), I was wheeled down to the NICU where I saw my perfect little baby boy hooked up to all kinds of wires. The guilt set in again. I thought for sure I had done something to cause this precious little baby to enter the world before he was ready. Maybe I ate the wrong foods or maybe I was on my feet too much and caused him stress. I didn't know for sure if it was my fault, but I felt that as his mother I should have done more for him. I never expected to feel the way I did when I saw *MY* child. I had never known what it meant to love somebody so wholeheartedly and unselfishly until he entered my life.

The next day we learned that he was having difficulty keeping anything in his stomach. He also was unable to suck, swallow and breathe at the same time so he had to be on a feeding tube. We learned quickly that our short stay in the NICU was going to be longer than we expected. He was diagnosed with Milk Soy Protein Intolerance (MSPI). This meant I could not nurse him for two weeks because that was how long it would take for any milk or soy protein to leave my breast milk. It also meant I had to be on a very strict and limited diet. He also was having problems with acid reflux. As if I didn't feel bad enough, now I was devastated that I wouldn't be able to nurse my precious baby. I was the first person in my whole family who even wanted to breastfeed and I felt as though my chance was going to be blown.

I sat with my baby boy for 12-13 hours a day. I held him all day because I was afraid he wouldn't know my voice, touch or smell. I only left him when I needed to pump or during shift changes when they wouldn't allow any visitors. I wanted to know everything that was going on with my baby. Leaving every night was the hardest thing I ever had to do. I cried the whole drive home because I felt like I was abandoning my baby. I would have stayed with him all night but I was afraid I would get sick and they would not let me into the NICU. I woke up religiously every two hours to pump. Most new parents don't sleep because their new baby keeps them awake. I would have given anything to be awakened by the sound of my baby's cry, not the alarm. So instead of waking up to feed him, I woke up to pump and cry while I looked at a photo album instead of at his precious little face.

After 17 days we finally got to bring him home. Right before it was time to leave, I started to panic. I had watched my little boy stop breathing while in the hospital and I was so afraid he would do it again. I was going through several different emotions: excitement, fear, wonder. I loved my little boy so much that I was determined to do everything I could to be the best mom. I had no idea what challenges and struggles lied ahead for me and my precious baby.

Within a day of being home, our sweet little boy turned into the devil. All he did was cry and cry. He didn't sleep a wink and was still bothered so much by his reflux that he threw up everywhere ... all the time. After a couple weeks of having my baby home, my feelings toward my perfect baby began to change. I didn't feel the unconditional love I had felt before. In fact, I didn't even want a baby anymore. I had so many expectations of what it was going to be like to have a new baby and NOTHING had been the way I expected it to be. It was not at all what I thought parenting would be like. I felt guilty because I dreaded being home alone with my baby. He literally cried *all* day long. I would try to walk away but it only lasted for a few minutes because I was afraid he would throw up and choke. My relationship with my husband was suffering because my husband didn't understand what I was going through. I wasn't ready for how much life was going to change when I became a mom. I guess I wasn't as ready to give up all of my 'me' time as I thought.

After some time, I had accepted that my life had changed. I realized that I had chosen to become a parent and I needed to give it my all. My little boy is almost four years old now and I can honestly say that he and his little sister, too, are the best things that have ever happened to me. I still get an aching feeling when I think about all the emotions I had toward my little boy when he came home from the hospital. I have been able to let go of some of the guilt because I realize now that I was put in a situation I couldn't have been prepared for. I had too many false expectations. I love my little boy more than life itself and am so thankful that God chose me to be his mother. I wouldn't trade this life for anything. It's Okay.

Maternity Leave Mayhem

I loved my first born dearly from the moment I held her. I never understood what people said about 'love at first sight' when you meet your child, until that precious little thing was laid in my arms. I couldn't wait for our months together at home, bonding and getting to know one another. I was so thankful I had three months of maternity leave and knew that I would enjoy every minute of it! Wait. Maybe not!

Some would call it colic, some would call it fussy, I just call it my most difficult time at home. Nothing I did would soothe her. Swing after swing, swaddle after swaddle and pacifier after pacifier. There was the shushing and the rocking and the lavender baths. *Nothing* seemed to calm her. I would be up night after night, hour after hour and visions of the 'never shake your baby' videos from the hospital would flash warning signs in my head. We very rarely had those lovey-dovey sweet bonding moments that the books talk about. Don't get me wrong, I loved her to pieces … I just don't think I really liked her.

I also didn't like being at home on maternity leave. How did the perfect pregnancy and perfect labor and delivery turn into this devilish thing who was my daughter? She seemed to hate me. I cringed at the thought of going out into public. I was always walking on egg shells, worried that her inner rage would shine through in front of others. And then, to top it all off, there were the comments. "Oh, what a sweet baby," and, "Enjoy every moment of this, it goes so fast!" I wanted it to go fast. I wanted to wish away this precious time that was anything but enjoyable. I wanted to shout at these people. *"Are you kidding me?* Enjoy what?" I did not understand how people did this more than once. Nor did I understand why people didn't head back to work as soon as they could walk out of the hospital.

I learned a valuable lesson from my first-born. I am not always going to like my children. I don't have to. I do love them dearly and my second child was nothing like my first. We did have those amazing moments that you read about. But, parenting is hard. And some moments are better than others. My struggles may be different than yours, but we all have them. Parenting is not always enjoyable and I will never assume that any parent is enjoying every minute. It's got to be the cumulative moments and love that really counts. It's Okay.

Stupid Snack

'Stupid' is not a word that is used in our house. I have hated that word for many years, even before I became an educator. I used to correct students at school for using that word and usually required them to repeat their sentence using a different, kinder phrase. I had vowed that my children would not use that word and *thought* that I had done a good job enforcing that notion.

Once our two oldest children hit the ages of six and five, it became more difficult to find cartoons that were still interesting to them. Sponge Bob Square Pants was an unfortunate show they could agree they would both enjoy. I held off on letting this be an option for many years, explaining that 'stupid' was a word Sponge Bob used and we didn't use that word in our house.

I ended up losing the Sponge Bob battle. It was not all the time, but the show definitely made it onto our TV more than once. At the time, our third child was three and, unfortunately, she took a great liking to the Sponge Bob character. Now, I know that Sponge Bob was not the root problem of my three-year-old's language, but she somehow had a newfound interest in using the 'stupid' word. How does it happen? How do we lose control as parents? I tried vinegar and soap, time-outs, redirection after redirection; nothing seemed to help. My daughter even lit a candle at church one week. When I asked her what she prayed for, she whispered in my ear that she prayed she would stop using the 'stupid' word. Even she didn't like the darn word.

There really is no good excuse for how the events all transpired that morning. But, unfortunately, they did. There was a battle about something. It was clothes or hair or teeth, who knows? The three-year-old was being particularly difficult. The older two were actually doing an awesome job, but I was going to be late for work and I needed HER to get moving. Some words were shared and I think a punch was thrown (by her) and she ended up in a time-out. I went up a few minutes later. Now, I was still going to be late and taking a time-out was not helping the tardiness. I was disappointed to be greeted by my angry daughter. "I hate this stupid family. You're such a stupid mom."

I stayed pretty calm. I gave her some more time and reminded her that we still needed to get her snack together for preschool. I encouraged her that she might want to finish her time-out quickly so she'd have time to eat breakfast and to get her snack. I asked her to come down for breakfast when she was calm and then we could get her snack together. Moments later, and before she was calm, she came down to the kitchen. We were scrambling to get things wrapped up so that we could walk out the door shortly.

I don't know what sparked her comments or why her attitude hadn't turned around, but she continued her bash on me and our family. "You're so stupid. I wish I wasn't even in this stupid family." I tried to redirect her, telling her I went ahead and got her snack ready for her so that she'd have something to eat at preschool. The verbal abuse by her would not stop. After several more 'stupid's' came out of her mouth, I lost any hope I had for keeping my cool.

"Oh yeah, well here's your STUPID snack," I shouted as I chucked her snack container on the floor as hard as I could. Now, to save myself a little shame, I guess I can say that I didn't chuck it at her. I looked like a raging animal. I sounded like a ridiculous hormonal teenager. But, alas, I was supposed to be the model parent. That morning I was anything but. Not only did I use the word I despise so dearly, but I broke the container that my darling's snack was in. The topper to all this is that the container wasn't just any container. It was a container that my three-year-old had bought *with her own money*.

The preschool teachers got quite a story that day—my three-year-old just had to share! I didn't hear anything from them, but I am sure they had doubts about my parenting skills. My three-year-old and I had a long heart-to-heart about the events that had transpired. I didn't make excuses for my behavior, but let her know how deeply she had hurt me with her words. I replaced the darn container and worked to make an example out of my childish behavior.

Many years later, this event has not left my child's mind. While I don't think she is traumatized by it, she was definitely affected by the fact that I was so angry I broke something very important to her. I am not perfect. I get angry. I yell and scream at times. I only hope the reflecting I do with my children after mistakes are made helps them to see that we are all human and every human here on earth makes mistakes ... even their mom! It's Okay.

Inconceivable Lies

Well, at least I am talking about my seven-year-old and not my husband. And my lies weren't about cheating or inappropriate behavior. They were about the Tooth Fairy. It was easy at first, being a super great fairy to my missing-tooth girl! But, after losing more than one tooth, things got a little hairy. Certainly I could have made my situation easier, less complicated, but that's not the kind of person I am; apparently that's not how I roll!

Tooth #1: She lost her first big tooth. This was a major event. The Tooth Fairy successfully made a visit and deposited a five dollar bill. We knew this wasn't the amount we were going to give for all of her teeth, but it was her first. We wanted to make it extraordinary and certainly this large amount would do the trick.

Tooth #2: The real tradition started here! I heard this great idea from someone. To use one of each coin amount: quarter, penny, nickel, and dime! GREAT! A new tradition began. I knew it was kind of a random amount, my husband thought it was stupid, but hey, it could be our tradition. It is so hard to create those traditions that are yours; those traditions that you actually start early enough in your children's lives and then continue on year after year. So, $0.41 it was. She was tickled to use her money counting skills to figure out her amount.

Tooth #3: Our tradition was in full force. Quarter, penny, nickel, dime; $0.41 again and beaming with pride for her coin counting abilities. This time she did it all on her own. She thought it was a little strange that this was what the Tooth Fairy left again, but I was able to convince her that this special amount was given to her as a unique offering.

Tooth #4: I may have been a little tired that night and the sleep deprivation had to have gotten in my way. I was already in bed when my hubby asked me if I took care of the tooth. Nope. Oops. I ran down the stairs, grabbed the quarter, penny, nickel and dime and placed them under her pillow. The next morning, she was super excited. "Mom, the Tooth Fairy left me $1.16!" Yeah right, she apparently couldn't count her coins yet. I asked her to let me see. Sure as you know what, there was a nickel, a dime, a penny and A SILVER DOLLAR. Ugh. "Well, I guess that tooth was worth more." I decided we could worry about this later. Many months would pass before her next tooth would arrive.

Tooth #5: This tooth took a while to come out. It gave me many months to ponder how to make up for my last tooth mishap. One day, shortly before losing her fifth tooth, my daughter came to me with information she had received from a friend. Apparently this little friend had written to the Tooth Fairy and the Tooth Fairy wrote her back about how different people have different fairies. These Tooth Fairies all come from different places and wear different clothes. Well, great idea. I can do that. So, I encouraged my little lady to write *her* Tooth Fairy a letter.

It was about midnight when I realized I had to come up with a letter back to my child. A friend was in town staying with us and went to bed laughing at me. I had decided to type the letter so she wouldn't recognize my handwriting. The only problem ... our printer ended up being out of ink. It was nearing one o'clock in the morning and I was ready to give up. So, I simply wrote on the back of my daughter's letter, "Have your mom check her e-mail." That way all my work in writing my daughter's letter wouldn't go undone. I attached the letter to my e-mail and hoped for the best.

The next morning, my daughter showed me the note and I pulled up my e-mail. Perfect! Well, the letter was elaborate. It had too many details. My friend reminded me that the reason she went to bed laughing was because I was making this too complicated! My daughter looked a little skeptical, but was excited to know that her fairy came from a Hawaiian island nicknamed the Friendly Isle, that she worked as a dentist by day and Tooth Fairy at night and that she wore regular clothes during the day but a shimmering pink dress that sparkled in the night light. Did I mention that I went over the top in the letter?????

I also made the mistake of just grabbing two one dollar bills. I didn't know what to give her. I didn't have it in me that night to come up with a new tradition. Why did I grab two? What was I thinking? I don't know. Anyway, the next morning, I assured her she got two dollars because of the note she wrote. Maybe that would set me up for the next tooth. By the way, my hubby was out of town for this whole adventure and agreed with my friend that I was an idiotic mother for trying to keep up on all this. "Couldn't you just have put a dollar under her pillow and wrote thanks for the letter?" I was bound and determined to prove to him that this was a good idea!

Tooth #6: Well, with the tradition destroyed and a skeptical child, I was at a loss for what to do with the sixth tooth. She thought she had swallowed her tooth, only to find it late the next night before falling asleep. She had already written a note telling the Tooth Fairy she was sorry she didn't have a tooth to leave, so the note later got crossed out and changed, letting the Tooth Fairy know that the tooth was miraculously found.

Not wanting to go into great detail or have another e-mailed note, I wrote with my left hand that I was happy she found the tooth! One dollar was left. I **suck** at this tradition thing.

Long story short, I was trying to do a good thing. I wanted a tradition. Sadly, not only did I destroy a tradition, but I left a trail of lies that I can't keep up with. I think she knows her mother is a screw-up, but continues to play the game excited that her Tooth Fairy leaves her something under the pillow. Now, I'm left with what to do for my next child. I think I'll just start fresh, say he has a different Tooth Fairy, get a stack of silver dollars and hand one over for every tooth lost????? It's Okay.

Final Thoughts

Life is difficult. Life is challenging. Life throws you curve ball after curve ball. In the end, it's really not about the hardships that have overwhelmed your life, but about your reaction to the fact that life happens. While living is anything but easy, it's important to remember that there is beauty around every corner, joy inside every human being, kind actions that will inspire you and gifts that every person has to share.

This book was written with the hope that you will find peace in the fact that you are not the only human being that has issues. You are not the only parent that dislikes your children some days. You are not alone in your struggles. You are not an isolated being that has no hope for turning your sadness into sarcasm. Mistakes happen by everyone, everywhere and by parents all over the globe.

While I hope that you found enjoyment in reading this book, I also hope that you are inspired to live more contently; okay with the fact that your mistakes can turn into miracles. Your horrible moments can be turned into monumental growth. You will mess up. You will struggle. You will forget to count your blessings. While all these things are true, my hope for you after reading this book is that you will

1. Judge others less
2. Offer support more
3. Share your story honestly
4. Get 'real' about your struggles

5. Find the balance that works for you
6. Not be afraid to ask for help
7. Give yourself the credit you deserve
8. Laugh big and laugh often
9. Appreciate the struggles that are yours
10. Be thankful for those that drive you most crazy

Thank you for sharing in my journey. It's been an amazing ride and I'm so glad you joined me for this part of the trip. You, too, can make a difference for others out there by sharing your own journeys. There are many more 'It's Okay' books to come.

For more information on upcoming books or to be a story contributor, visit www.itsokaybooks.com.

Future books in the works

That's Okay, Too
More real stories about this thing we call parenting

It's Okay
Let's get real about this thing we call marriage

It's Okay
Let's get real about getting old

It's Okay
Let's get real about the daily grind

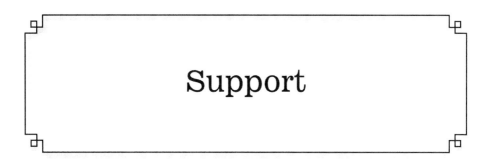

Support

For those of you reading this book that feel you are in need of more support than just a good laugh or the idea that you are not alone in your struggles; I highly recommend seeking professional assistance. Though I do not know your personal struggles, I know that everyone can benefit from talking with someone they trust. Professional help is available and you may truly need it. You are not a failure because you need help. You should feel proud of yourself for recognizing that you might have more in your life than you can handle alone.

The resources mentioned below are just a small start to an abundance of possibilities in your area. When searching for help, it is critical to find someone that you feel confident and comfortable working with. It's okay to need help. It's not okay to avoid seeking assistance when you are in dire need. Best wishes.

American Academy of Pediatrics, www.aap.org
La Leche League International, www.lalecheleague.org
Postpartum Support International, www.postpartum.net
National Alcoholism and Substance Abuse Information Center, www.addictioncareoptions.com
National Institute of Mental Health, www.nimh.nih.gov
Substance Abuse and Mental Health Services Administration, www.samhsa.gov
Psychology Today, www.psychologytoday.com

About the Author

I thought after reading this book, you might want to know a little bit about the lady who compiled it all! As you know, my name is Teresa Hamilton. I am the mother of four beautiful children and the wife of Tim Hamilton. We have been married for eight years and I believe that we have accomplished a great deal in our short marriage. I'd like to tell you that experiencing the birth of our four babies and the career paths that have come and gone have all been rosy and perfect. This is not the case. Our life is challenging, just like many of you who are reading this book. Though our challenges are different than yours, they still exist.

I came up with the idea of this book because I felt as though I had so many blessings in my life, but I was struggling to appreciate and enjoy them. I was working full time when the thought, 'It's Okay,' first crossed my mind. It was interesting how many friends and family members that I talked to seemed to feel the same way I was feeling; overwhelmed and full of guilt. People loved the idea of sharing the stories that we are often too ashamed to admit to. It's rejuvenating to know that you are not the only one!

Keeping up with life means different things to different people! Nonetheless, life moves along with expectations the whole way. Whether it's cleaning the house, getting the groceries, doing the bills, caring for a family, perfecting a career, changing a career, etc., the fact remains that life requires that we participate in various ways in order to be able to fulfill our basic needs.

When we start defining 'who' we really are, things become difficult. Where do we spend our time? Is it at work? Is that what defines us? Surely the time we have spent preparing for the job we have should amount to something. And without a job, we have no money to participate in the different activities life throws at us. Do we define ourselves by our family or our religious beliefs or our hobbies or the things we are good at?

Needing a good balance in life is critical for personal success. What, then, defines balance? This definition varies from person to person and even year to year. Last year, after struggling through a year of full-time work with four children six and under, my balance was as out of whack as it could be. I needed something, but didn't know what. I wasn't enjoying my children, my husband, my messy house, my quick-as-could-be meals or my job. I had always LOVED working in the education field and loved the work I did as an elementary counselor. I didn't know if giving all that up would help me achieve my needed balance?

Having no time to actually enjoy the things that were important to me in life became a priority. I quit my job in the hopes that I could reevaluate our family priorities and enjoy a little of what we had been blessed with. This, of course, did not come without sacrifice. I had to give up some of the other things that actually provided me with balance in previous years. It's funny to me that I put in over nine years of graduate and post-graduate work, only to take on the job of a stay-at-home mom, which I was given zero training or preparation for (kind of scary when you think about it, really)!

Learning to be okay with not being able to 'do it all' really put me at ease. I've always been able to tackle life with full force, so stepping back, slowing down and even admitting to needing less stress in my life was not easy. I did not fail and some might even say that I was more of a winner for the decision I made to stay at home. Whatever you think, it's really okay, because it was what was best for me (I haven't always been in this place ... able to let go of what others think ☺)!

Our family still struggles. Our family still has out-of-control moments. Our family still yells and squabbles and even has wrestling matches occasionally. But, I'm less likely to fly off the handle than I was last year. It's okay! When I do fly off the handle, it's okay! I'm going to mess up, I'm not going to be perfect and my kids are going to be kids.

t really is okay. My mantra has helped keep me sane and believing that made the right choice.

My hope is that as you read through the stories in this book, you egan to look at your parenting journey or the life journey you are currently traveling, and realize that sometimes life isn't all it's cracked up .o be! That's okay. Try to enjoy the moments you have, try to give yourself permission to mess up, and try to laugh at the crazy things that happen in life (because crazy things do happen). Know that things are going to go wrong, that you can't control everything happening around you and that the only person you have complete control over is yourself. Hey, it's okay.

CPSIA information can be obtained at www.ICGtesting.com
Printed in the USA
LVOW10s0945180813

348442LV00017B/657/P